Political Violence in South

Political Violence in South Africa

John Kane-Berman

SOUTH AFRICAN INSTITUTE OF RACE RELATIONS
JOHANNESBURG
1993

In these references the **Survey** means the **Race Relations Survey** (previously **Survey of Race Relations in South Africa**), published by the South African Institute of Race Relations annually since 1936. The **Surveys** are referred to by the year under review, not the year of publication, which may be the following year. **Race Relations News** is the Institute's quarterly bulletin. References to **Fast Facts** are to a concise monthly publication dealing with current events, also published by the Institute.

Published by the South African Institute of Race Relations
Auden House, 68 De Korte Street
Braamfontein, Johannesburg, 2001 South Africa

PD11/93
ISBN 0-86982-434-1

Printed and bound by Galvin & Sales

Acknowledgements

As the references indicate, this booklet draws on the work of research and public affairs staff at the South African Institute of Race Relations. My thanks are due to them, as well as to the staff of the Institute's Hofmeyr library, in particular Ellen Potter and Alfred Nkungu. I am also grateful to Robin Harvey, Anne Pogrund, Walter Saunders, Susan Thompson, and Jill Wentzel for reading the manuscript and making comments which helped improve it. I am further indebted to Penny Parks for her patience in typing numerous drafts.

Over thy wounds now do I prophesy, –
A curse shall light upon the limbs of men;
Domestic fury and fierce civil strife,
Shall cumber all the parts of Italy;
Blood and destruction shall be so in use,
That mothers shall but smile when they behold
Their infants quarter'd with the hands of war;
And Caesar's spirit, ranging for revenge,
Shall in these confines with a monarch's voice
Cry 'Havoc!' and let slip the dogs of war...
Now let it work. Mischief, thou art afoot,
Take thou what course thou wilt!

– Mark Antony in *Julius Caesar*, Act III, Scenes 1 and 2

Lay not that flattering unction to your soul
That not your trespass but my madness speaks.

– Hamlet in *Hamlet*, Act IV, Scene 4

Contents

Overview: 40-year perspective

For much of the last four decades South Africa has in a sense been two countries in one. Whites, generally speaking, lived under a democratic system, while blacks were subject to the dictatorial powers of a massive, coercive, bureaucratic apparatus.

As many people predicted, repression bred violent reaction. Some thirty or more years ago, the African National Congress (ANC) and the Pan-Africanist Congress (PAC) were banned, a sabotage campaign was launched, Mr Nelson Mandela was jailed, and 'armed struggle' was planned from bases in neighbouring states set up by the two banned movements.[1] Internal repression thus had the unexpected consequence that it bred externally-based insurgency. Probably only a few people believed that sabotage, or even the killing of civilians by such things as car bombs, could overthrow the government. These strategies were designed rather to erode the white support base of the state.

By the mid 1970s, however, the 'armed struggle' had effectively come to a halt. Very little was heard of the ANC, which appears to have been as surprised by the outbreak of violence in Soweto on 16th June 1976 as was the government itself, which ignored all warnings about the tension that was building up in the township over its policy of forcing black schoolchildren to study through the medium of Afrikaans, rejected by them as the language of the oppressor. Although the 1976/77 upheavals drew their inspiration from black consciousness, the ANC and the South African Communist Party were the main beneficiaries. When several thousand youngsters fled Soweto and other townships in the second half of 1976 the South African organisation best equipped to receive them outside the country was the ANC. The security police said that the growth in guerrilla activity inside the country in 1977 was the 'natural result' of the mass exodus of blacks from South Africa after June 1976. The police predicted, accurately, that the number of insurgents would increase[2] as the exiles, having received military training from the ANC (and, to a lesser extent, the PAC), returned home to wage the 'armed struggle'.

In the 1980s, armed struggle was broadened into 'people's war'. The campaign gathered momentum in protests against the implementation of the new tricameral constitution in September 1984. One of the earliest disturbances occurred in the black township of Sebokeng in the Vaal Triangle in the first week of September that year, at the same time as the tricameral parliament first met and its chief architect, Mr P W Botha, was elevated from prime minister to state president.

Whereas in 1976 several thousand black youngsters had fled South Africa, this time round much of the militant youth stayed in the country, mainly because, in terms of the Nkomati Accord signed in March 1984, Mozambique agreed to stop sheltering South African insurgents and South Africa agreed to stop attacking Mozambique. Here was another unexpected consequence. Military action by South Africa against neighbouring states undermined externally-based armed struggle and thereby helped to fuel internal resistance.

Yet another unexpected consequence loomed. The people's war, directed in theory against the state, in fact helped to unleash massive violence within black communities. Black people, who were the victims of apartheid itself, became also the victims of the struggle against apartheid. This study tries to show how this happened.

Introduction

Statistics

By the end of May 1993, the total number of fatalities in political violence since its outbreak in September 1984 was 15 843, nearly two thirds of them since the beginning of 1990.[3]

Most violent deaths nevertheless arise not from politics but from ordinary crime. In 1991, for example, there were nearly 14 700 murders, of which about 80% appeared to be unrelated to political questions. In 1992, according to official figures, 88% of murders were apparently not politically related. In 1983–1992, during which period there were more than 15 000 political fatalities, there were more than 118 000 murders altogether.[4] Even though the dividing line between the different types of violence is sometimes blurred, this study will concentrate on political violence.

Socio-economic factors

Political violence is partly rooted in poverty, squalor, and unemployment, problems which cannot be dealt with in the short term. Also, one should beware of blaming the violence too strongly on socio-economic factors. Personal income per head in the Pretoria/Witwatersrand/Vereeniging (PWV) area is more than double the national average, but this region alone has at times accounted for half the violence in the country.[5] There are also localised causes, such as the battle for market share among taxi owners.[6]

Violence and the State

National Party policies

The original cause of the violence was the National Party (NP) government. When black people demonstrated against the pass laws at Sharpeville in 1960, it mowed them down with sten guns.[7] When schoolchildren demonstrated against Bantu Education in Soweto in 1976, it shot them down too. It banned and house arrested people after stigmatising many of them as communists, and several dozen of them it beat to death or drove to suicide in detention.[8] Not content with banning people it closed down newspapers and banned numerous political organisations.[9] The more it drove black opposition underground and into acts of desperation and violence, the bigger its majorities got in parliament. During the worst of these years – the 1960s – the whites who objected to all of this were so few in number that they managed to scrape together enough votes to send precisely one MP to Cape Town – Mrs Helen Suzman. When she opposed some of the worst of the detention laws, she did so alone, for the then official opposition, the United Party (UP), was more concerned with fighting elections on slogans like 'Want TV? Vote UP'. For most of the time all these outrages against black people had the backing, implicit or explicit, of some of the business community, the Afrikaans press, and, of course, very important in a supposedly God-fearing country, the Dutch Reformed Churches. Those few clerics who objected, like Ds Beyers Naudé and Professor Albert Geyser,[10] were branded as heretics. Among the organisations stigmatised was the South African Institute of Race Relations,[11] whose 60 years of annual **Surveys** and other publications[12] are the Encyclopaedia Britannica of the apartheid system. They constitute a meticulous, factual, and damning indictment, unrivalled anywhere.

The darkest days of apartheid are gone,[13] but the legacy and the wounds remain. They cannot be eliminated by a single speech, no matter how decisive a break State President F W de Klerk tried to make with the past when he opened parliament on 2nd February 1990. The NP's track record helps to explain why so many people believe the allegations that the government is orchestrating a 'third force' consisting of the South African Police (SAP), the South African Defence Force (SADF), the Inkatha Freedom Party (IFP), vigilantes, and miscellaneous 'hit squads' to destroy the African National Congress (ANC).[14] The theory has such wide currency both in South Africa and abroad that it merits examination in some detail.

The 'third force' theory

The president of the ANC, Mr Nelson Mandela, has been among those making the accusations. For example, he said in October 1991 that Mr de Klerk had 'let loose his hounds against the people'.[15] In an address on 15th July 1992 to the United Nations Security Council in the wake of the Boipatong massacre, in which more than 40 people were killed, allegedly by IFP-supporting hostel residents, a month previously, Mr Mandela spoke of a strategy of 'state terrorism' in which the IFP had 'permitted itself to become an extension of the Pretoria regime, its instrument and surrogate'. In December 1992, Mr Mandela referred to 'the fact that the state security services, using certain black organisations, have been responsible for the death of no less than 15 000 people since 1984'.[16]

The Commission of Inquiry Regarding the Prevention of Public Violence and Intimidation (the Goldstone Commission), which was established in 1991, has said no evidence has been submitted to it to substantiate accusations that the government is orchestrating violence,[17] but they persist. Speaking in September 1992 Mr Chris Hani, former chief of staff of Umkhonto we Sizwe, the military wing of the ANC, and then general secretary of the South African Communist Party (SACP), said that the government was pursuing a twin-track strategy which involved negotiation with the ANC and 'at the same time deliberate [and] violent destabilisation' of its forces. Mr Hani said that whereas the ANC-led alliance had not deployed violence strategically since 1990, the government was deploying it systematically as 'a central component of a political strategy' making use of proxy forces including 'Contras, Unitas, Renamos, Askaris, Lesotho Liberation Armies, the Ciskei Defence Force etc backed up by small, special forces and seconded officers from the main army'. Mr Hani went on to say that violence – in train massacres, for example – was being 'switched on and off', and that 80% of the victims were ANC members or supporters. The government's objective was political rather than military, he said. Its aim was to 'impose a political settlement on a war-weary people'.[18]

Such allegations should not lightly be dismissed. The conviction in 1992 of a white police officer, Captain Brian Mitchell, and four black non-commissioned officers for the massacre of 11 people in December 1988 in the village of Trust Feed near Greytown in the Natal Midlands was not the first time black and white policemen had been found guilty of murder. The murders were, moreover, part of a strategy to promote the IFP at the expense of the then-banned ANC's de facto internal ally, the United Democratic Front (UDF) (although the killers murdered IFP supporters by mistake). The judge also found that the initial police investigation into the Trust Feed massacre was so incompetent as to suggest an attempt at concealment, possibly in top police ranks. He called for an independent inquiry into the investigation and the possible involvement of police officers in 'counter-revolutionary strategies'.[19]

In another case, seven IFP members were acquitted for lack of evidence on 38 counts of murder at a massacre at an ANC funeral vigil in Sebokeng in 1991. The judge said the police should have tried harder to find incriminating evidence, although he also pointed out that the police had said that the ANC had prevented them from speaking to some of the witnesses.[20] The Association of Law Societies found it necessary to criticise the fact that a member of the KwaZulu police was released from prison in February 1992 after serving less than a year of a 27-year sentence for murder despite having been described by the judge as a 'beast in policeman's clothing' who seemed to enjoy his reputation as a 'hit man' and the fear this caused in the KwaMashu township outside Durban.[21] Other members of the IFP, including a KwaZulu deputy minister, have been convicted of murder.[22] In April 1993 four IFP members were convicted of smuggling arms into South Africa from Mozambique.[23]

Yet another cause for suspicion is the publication of a document implicating the State Security Council and top military officers in the 'permanent removal' – and alleged murder – of political activists, among them Mr Matthew Goniwe, in the Eastern Cape in 1985.[24] At the time of writing, an inquest into the murders was in progress.[25] The government's insistence in October 1992 on legislation that could be used to indemnify state employees (and others) who may have committed acts of violence has done little to diminish suspicions, especially since details of the crimes in question may be kept secret.[26]

After seizing a number of files from a covert military operations unit on 11th November 1992, the Goldstone Commission said that 'highly placed members of military intelligence' had been party to the employment of Mr Ferdi Barnard, 'a notorious former member of the Civil Co-operation Bureau' (CCB), to obtain information about Umkhonto we Sizwe, and in particular its involvement in crime. The chairman of the commission, Mr Justice Richard Goldstone, said that Mr Barnard had two previous convictions for murder, one for attempted murder, and three for theft, and that the SADF had denied employing him when this was 'quite untrue'.[27]

Mr Barnard was alleged in the press to have been involved in the murder of a UDF activist and university lecturer, Dr David Webster, in May 1989. In January 1993, however, Mr Justice Michael Stegmann came to the rather unsatisfactory conclusion that responsibility for the crime could not be pinned on any person in particular. Although Dr Webster's death had been brought about by acts constituting a conspiracy to murder, Judge Stegmann said, it could not be conclusively proved that Dr Webster had been an 'officially sanctioned CCB project' or that the organisation or any of its members had killed him. This was despite the fact that evidence before him had indicated that the CCB included as part of its programme the proposed elimination of certain 'targeted' people. Evidence incriminating Mr Barnard was circumstantial, the judge said, and he was 'at this stage entitled to the benefit of the doubt'. Judge Stegmann added, 'For the present the truth has not been brought to light.'[28]

The CCB, which was formally constituted under that name in 1986 in the defence force, was widely suspected of murdering ANC supporters and other anti-apartheid activists. It was formally disbanded in 1990, various attempts to penetrate the secrecy surrounding its activities having failed, partly as a result of the disappearance of some of its records.[29] At the time of writing it seemed likely that many of the mysterious deaths of anti-apartheid activists down the years would never be finally cleared up. After the Webster finding, an ANC official said the organisation reserved the right to re-open all inquests into political assassinations when it came to power.[30]

Mr de Klerk has admitted the involvement of security force members in violence. While denying the existence of any 'third force', he said in November 1992 that 'obviously there might be individuals who have their own agendas'. A month later, announcing that 23 senior officers of thc defence force were being retired or sent on leave, following investigations by the Goldstone Commission and by the SADF's chief of staff, Mr de Klerk said SADF personnel had been or were still involved in illegal activities, including, apparently, activities that 'led to the deaths of people'. The ANC interpreted this statement as confirming its contention that there was a 'third force' operating within the security forces, but Mr de Klerk repeated his denial of such a force and stated that only a limited number of persons and a few units were involved. At the time of writing is was not clear whether subsequent investigations would result in prosecutions.[31]

The *Sunday Star* reported soon after the departure of the 23 officers that more than 60 former Rhodesians had been dismissed in the 'latest government purge' of military intelligence. One was quoted as saying, 'They used us over all those years. They were happy to get us to carry out their dirty work. Who do you think they used to do eliminations? And now they want to dump us.' The newspaper said that the ex-Rhodesians were planning to bring lawsuits against the government and the SADF.[32] A former managing director of the CCB, Colonel Joe Verster, said nobody in the organisation had done anything without authority.[33]

More is known about shootings by the police than about what military personnel may have done. The police have killed more than 560 black people in political demonstrations since the shootings at Sharpeville in 1960, and possibly as many as 660. Most of these were shot dead, some in the back, in the riots in Soweto and elsewhere which began on 16th June 1976.[34]

As far as is known, no top-ranking police officer or politician has paid the price for the Sharpeville or Soweto or any other police shootings. Instead of firing the general or the minister, National Party governments have put indemnity legislation through parliament. Almost inevitably, a culture developed in which some members of the police force thought themselves above the law.

Nor is it surprising that several dozen people have died in detention under security laws.

The first such death on record is that of Mr Solwandle Looksmart Ngudle, a trade unionist and ANC member who was said to have committed suicide by hanging himself in Pretoria in September 1963. Six years ago the Institute published a study of deaths in detention, listing across several columns the name, date of death, place, age, and so on. There are 63 names on this list between 1963 and 1984. One column is headed 'Criminal Proceedings'. The word 'no' appears no fewer than 59 times in this column.[35] If governments enact laws empowering policemen to detain people indefinitely beyond the reach of lawyers, courts, private doctors, families and friends, and those people keep dying and very few prosecutions are brought against the police, then the message that the government is in effect sending to the security police is that it is acceptable to torture people. How different South Africa's history might have been if Mr John Vorster, minister of justice in 1963, had been forced to resign when Mr Ngudle died. Mr Ngudle might have been the only South African to die in this way.

Even though the powers of the police to detain people without trial have been severely curtailed (from an indefinite period to a maximum of ten days), people continue to die at a high rate in police custody – 153 in 1991 and 210 in 1992, according to the government's own figures,[36] many of them people arrested on suspicion of offences unrelated to politics.

South Africa has a problem of lawless and proven criminal behaviour on the part of policemen, 1 871 of whom were convicted of criminal offences in 1991 (while 5 314 were disciplined for departmental offences).[37]

The 'third force' theory is plausible from a political point of view. Grand apartheid sought to divide and rule the black population, and for the National Party to seek an alliance with the more conservative black parties against the radicals and then to exploit ethnicity to undermine other parties would have a kind of logic about it. Suspicions are reinforced by the secret funding of the IFP and an IFP-linked trade union, the fact that the police have been less than zealous in preventing IFP members from brandishing dangerous weapons in public, and the fact that the Goldstone Commission found it necessary to take the government to task for inadequately implementing its recommendations to curb this practice.[38]

Scrutinising the 'third force' theory

It is necessary to probe a little more deeply into some of the theories or reports which, explicitly or implicitly, attribute violence in South Africa almost exclusively to the state or even see violence as the result of a government strategy to destroy its opponents.

The Community Agency for Social Enquiry (Case) and a group known as the Human Rights Commission (HRC) have claimed that the government switches violence on and off at 'key moments'. They say it turns violence up when it would weaken the ANC and its allies. The HRC and Case thus claim that violence is turned up during ANC conferences and campaigns. Their reports fail to mention several conferences and campaigns when violence dropped. The HRC and Case further argue that the government switches violence off when Mr de Klerk travels abroad. Their reports fail to mention overseas trips by the state president that coincide with increases in violence. Case says that the 'government-sponsored peace conference in June [1991], boycotted by the liberation movements but attended by Inkatha, saw a major diminution of violence'. June 1991 did see a major drop in violence. But the conference was in May 1991 – a month which, according to Case's own figures, had the third highest incidence of fatalities during the period under consideration.[39] A forensic specialist at the medical school of the University of Natal involved with autopsies of victims of violence in Natal said he had done a week-by-week analysis of incidents of violence and also of political developments from 1989 to 1992 but had found no correlation between the two.[40]

The HRC has also contended that 'vigilante-related causes' accounted for 83% of all politically-related deaths in one 12-month period. Vigilantes were said to be acting 'at the government's command'.[41] But the HRC used the term 'vigilante-related action' in such a way as to blame on 'vigilantes' not only attacks which they may themselves have carried out but also attacks in which 'vigilantes' were killed. This definition was so wide as to tar both victims and perpetrators of violence with the same brush.[42] In one report the HRC even blamed 'vigilantes'[43] for murders that by its own admission were carried out by 'unidentified' and 'unknown' attackers. Without citing evidence it blamed vigilantes for no fewer than 49 killings in a single month, among them necklace executions, when this method of killing is often employed by militant 'comrades' rather than by 'vigilantes'. Subsequent to criticism by the Institute of the attempts to blame nearly all violence on 'vigilantes', the HRC stopped using this categorisation. Whereas the HRC said 71,3% of all politically related fatalities in 1992 were 'vigilante-related', and that 'private armies' of vigilantes 'of late have considerably widened the scope of their attacks to destabilise township communities at large', its report for February 1993 made no mention of vigilantes. Most fatalities (76%) were now said to have occurred in 'general incidents'.[44]

In July 1992 the HRC issued a report on massacres since 1990, among them 11 massacres in Natal since July that year. One of the massacres occurred in June 1991 in Richmond in the Natal Midlands. According to the commission, 16 ANC supporters were killed by the IFP on this occasion.[45] However, there was another massacre in Richmond three months before that, at the beginning of April. On this occasion not 16 but double that number of people were killed, most of them apparently IFP supporters.[46] The HRC makes no mention of this massacre, even though it says it looked into its records of more than 5 000 politically-related incidents and even though it defines a massacre as an incident in which ten or more people died.

Not only is the report selective in which massacres it mentions, but it in effect pronounces certain parties guilty of genocide on the basis of what it describes as media reports of 'allegations or deductions sometimes corroborated by legal evidence'. No court would use such methodology to convict even a minor offender.[47]

A book on 'apartheid death squads', published by a journalist, Mr Jacques Pauw, in 1991 contains a list of 225 'political assassinations of anti-apartheid activists' between February 1971 and February 1991. Mr Mandela has relied on this list to back his accusations that Mr de Klerk is an accomplice to murder.[48] It is almost certain that 'hit squads' exist. Captain Mitchell and his four subordinates could be described as one, although there is so far no evidence that they were acting on higher orders. Dr Webster may also have been a victim. Given the gravity of the allegations sometimes made about 'hit squads', however, it is striking that some of the assumptions on which the allegations rest are dubious and some of the information incorrect.

For example, the last victim listed in the book on 'apartheid death squads'[49] is Chief Mhlabunzima Maphumulo and his alleged killer is listed as one Sipho Madlala. Mr Madlala claimed to have been attached to the military police since 1986, that the murder had been plotted from the Alexandra Road police station in Pietermaritzburg, and that members of the hit squad of which he was part had each been given R5 000 for their part in the murder. The ANC said Mr Madlala had shown that government-controlled hit squads continued to assassinate people to 'stoke the flames of conflict and lay the blame at the door of Inkatha'. In the event, Mr Justice Page found that unknown people were responsible for the killing and that no reliance could be placed on Mr Madlala's story, which had been contradicted by every other witness and a 'vast body of documentary evidence'. The evidence of a second witness who claimed to be a 'hit squad' member was found to be 'appalling' and 'even worse' than that of Mr Madlala.[50]

Mr Pauw's list describes as 'unknown' the killer of Mr Saul Mkhize, who was shot dead in April 1983 at Driefontein near Piet Retief in the south-eastern Transvaal. However, the man who shot him was a 21-year-old police constable called Johannes Andries Nienaber whose photograph appeared in the press and who was acquitted a year later on a murder charge when the circuit court in Volksrust accepted his plea of self-defence — a verdict greeted with outrage. Mr Mkhize was shot dead in broad daylight in front of a large number of witnesses by an easily identifiable policeman wearing a uniform – not the way a 'hit squad' would operate.[51]

The HRC attributed the murder of Mr Andre de Villiers in Addo in the eastern Cape in August 1992 to 'hit squads', which it defined as 'faceless professional hitmen whose objective is to assassinate identified political figures and/or cripple anti-apartheid organisations'. In April 1993 one member of Umkhonto we Sizwe and another man were convicted of the murder.[52]

The HRC and Case reports and the 225-name list mentioned above are not the only documents that are open to question. In June 1992 Amnesty International produced a report which correctly quoted the Goldstone Commission as saying it had received evidence of police bias towards the IFP at the time of a massacre in Bruntville near Mooi River in Natal in December 1991, but failed to mention the Commission's *finding* that there was no unlawful conduct by the police.[53]

Similarly, a press release issued after a visit to South Africa in 1992 by the International Commission of Jurists (ICJ) carries a section headed 'dangerous weapons' but this section makes no mention of any weapons other than 'lethal traditional weapons' carried by members of the IFP. Indeed, nowhere in the ICJ's press release is there any reference to any other particular kind of weapon, a surprising omission in view of the fact that most incidents of violence involve firearms, petrol bombs, and hand grenades.[54] The ICJ calls for hostel residents to be disarmed but makes no recommendation that anyone else should be. The ICJ describes the KwaZulu police as a private army. No reference is made to any other private army. Like Amnesty, the ICJ quotes selectively from the Goldstone Commission and fails to mention its finding that the police were not to blame for the Bruntville violence.[55]

Amnesty, the ICJ, the HRC, and Case all have in common the view that violence is to be blamed mainly, if not almost entirely, on the government and the IFP. The involvement of both of these in violence is beyond question. However, one of the other things that Amnesty, the ICJ, the HRC, and Case have in common is that they fail to deal with violence directed against agents of the government and the IFP. Indeed, the problem with their reports, and with the 'third force' theories, is not what they do explain but what they do not explain. They do not explain why, according to the IFP, more that 1 000 of its members have been killed in violent attacks, why 275 of its office-bearers and leaders have been assassinated since 1985, or why the police have made so few arrests in connection with these killings, which the IFP describes as 'serial murders'.[56] Nor do these theories explain the violence directed against the police, nearly 700 of whom have been killed on duty in the last six years (although not necessarily always in political situations).[57]

The 'third force' theory has been doggedly promoted by *The Weekly Mail*. In an issue in July 1992 it ran an editorial attacking first as 'meaningless' and then as 'political' Mr Justice Goldstone's statement that 'no evidence' had been submitted to his commission 'which in any way justifies allegations of any direct complicity in or planning of current violence by the state president, any member of the cabinet, or any highly-placed officer in the South African Police or Defence Force'. The editorial stated: 'This newspaper for one has spent a great deal of time, energy and money assisting Justice Goldstone in his investigations.'[58] *The Weekly Mail* was nevertheless unable to provide proof. One of the co-editors of the paper admitted in August 1992 that its 'third force' allegations were based on 'patchy evidence' which is 'not always reliable'.[59]

Two other journalists who have written about the 'third force', Messrs Jacques Pauw and Shaun Johnson, said in August 1992 that the only real evidence forthcoming was the Trust Feed case – which was finally broken by a determined police officer. The definition of 'third force' then began to be changed – 'third force activities' would now be 'any illegal activities which have the effect of stoking violence and instability'.[60] This definition of the 'third force' is radically different from some of the earlier versions, which depicted the 'third force' as acting upon the command of the government itself. On the new definition Umkhonto we Sizwe, the Congress of South African Trade Unions (Cosatu), the ANC and the SACP join the IFP, the SAP, and the SADF in the 'third force'. The term becomes so wide as to lose all meaning – rather like Mr Vorster's definition of 'terrorist'. Mr Vorster also introduced laws to presume guilt until innocence was proved.[61] On this too the left is beginning to resemble the right. *The Weekly Mail*'s rebuke to Mr Justice Goldstone was, in effect, saying to him, 'We have already pronounced these people guilty. Why do you bring up such a "meaningless" factor as our inability to produce evidence?'

It should nevertheless be borne in mind that governments involved in covert or criminal activity can use further such activity to cover their tracks. Some of the covert operations of NP governments have been exposed over the years,[62] but there may be others as yet uncovered. It is conceivable that the 'third force' contains agents provocateurs who are killing IFP members and policemen by the hundred in order to provoke the IFP and the police into acts of violent retaliation against communities of ANC supporters. This would set up a vicious circle of attack and counter-attack which becomes self-perpetuating. It has been argued that this violence would in turn serve the interests of the government by derailing negotiations leading to majority rule and so leave the NP in power. So Machiavellian a strategy would be compatible with the known dishonesty, corruption, and brutality of apartheid rule, so it is as well to keep an open mind.

It is consistent with the NP's divide-and-rule policy that it might have sought, as a matter of deliberate strategy, to foment conflict between the ANC/UDF/Cosatu alliance on the one hand and the IFP on the other. An alliance between the ANC and the IFP would have presented a formidable challenge to the NP in constitutional negotiations. Instead, the ANC and the IFP have been at loggerheads. However, the theory that the conflict between the ANC and the IFP has been fomented by the government in order to weaken the ANC at the negotiating table overlooks the fact that the conflict goes back to the 1970s – long before the NP ever contemplated negotiations with the ANC. At that time NP policy was to hive off all ten of the homelands into constitutional independence of the rest of South Africa, not negotiate with black organisations for black people to be brought into parliament.

Without dismissing the possibility that a state-orchestrated 'third force' strategy does exist, this paper will put forward another explanation of the violence. Since it relies in part on material which could not lawfully be published in South African newspapers prior to 2nd February 1990, it will require more elaboration than the 'third force' theory, which has had such wide currency in the local and foreign media.

This explanation is put forward not as an academic exercise but because a full understanding of the violence and the dynamic that continues to drive it is a pre-condition of bringing it to an end. The explanation will widen the picture, by adding to it what the 'third force' theories usually omit – the strategies adopted in the struggle against apartheid, and the moral climate in which they were adopted.

Violence: the wider picture

Changing patterns of violence

It is instructive to begin by comparing the violence of the 1980s and 1990s with that of the 1970s.

Between June 1976 and October 1977, 700 people died – an average of 44 people a month. From the upsurge in September 1984 until the end of 1989, the average monthly death toll was almost double – 86. The violence of the 1980s was thus more intense than that of the 1970s. The 1990s have been even worse. In the whole of the period between September 1984 and the end of 1989 – for more than five years – the monthly level of political fatalities exceeded 200 no more than four times. From December 1989 to May 1990 – for six consecutive months – it was consistently above 200. In March 1990, for the first time ever, the level rose not only above 300 but also above 400 – to 458. This was the month after Mr de Klerk deregulated black politics in his now-celebrated speech.

Although most of the deaths in the disturbances in Soweto and elsewhere in 1976 and 1977 were at the hands of the police,[63] in the later 1980s and 1990s conflict between different groups of black people has been a major cause of fatalities. The Institute thus reported early in 1986 that 'attacks by some blacks against other blacks and conflict between different black groups...accounted for an increasing proportion of fatalities as (1985) progressed, the proportion accounted for by security forces diminishing'.[64] In 1985, security forces accounted for two thirds of fatalities and conflict within the black community for one third, but by 1987 the proportions were the other way round.[65]

The action of the police in 1976 gave major impetus to the violence of the 1980s. Although the judicial commission of inquiry into the Soweto violence in 1976 (the Cillie Commission) found the shootings to have been justified, the present writer's research for a book on the Soweto upheavals led him to the conclusion that the rioting might not have erupted had the police not opened fire on a basically peaceful crowd of marching schoolchildren on 16th June.[66]

Discussing that day in a newspaper article in February 1991, Mr Hani said:

> 'As usual in our country, if the police had not over-reacted that revolt would not have shaken the world. But the response of the police to a really peaceful demonstration by students – the violent response – spread to other parts of the country and impacted on the world. This was a turning point in terms of the militant struggle in our country. From then there was no looking back, we latched on. For the first time we had conditions where the young people were angry and where they had experienced the brutality and atrocities that had been perpetrated against them by the police and they were ready to join Umkhonto we Sizwe. Recruiting began to spread at a real pace now and we received more recruits in that year than we received in all the years when I had been in the country. Then the structures which we had built up inside the country began to spread rapidly and we stepped up recruiting, especially from the eastern Cape. There had been no cadres from the eastern Cape going out because of the distances but now they began to flood to Lesotho, coming from the eastern Cape, from the Free State, everywhere.'[67]

Mr Hani was correct when he said the shootings were a 'turning point'. However, the consequences went beyond a greater influx of youth into Umkhonto we Sizwe. An equally important result was the birth of a new type of township youth, inside and outside the ANC's military formations. The explosive reaction of all these youngsters in 1976 was turned within a few years into the major revolutionary impulse, which, fuelled by steadily rising unemployment, characterised the ferocious 'people's war' of the 1980s and early 1990s. The influence of the South African Communist Party (SACP) appears to have been important here. Without it, an ANC official said, 'we would have become just a black consciousness party'.[68]

In the last few years firearms have been used with increasing frequency in political violence. For example, it was reported in May

1993 that the number of autopsies performed in Durban on people who died of stab wounds dropped from 521 in 1989 to 366 in 1992, while the number of autopsies performed on victims of gunshot wounds increased from 354 to 1 109.

Police statistics were reported to show that altogether 777 people had been killed by AK47 assault rifles since 1988, 373 of them in the first nine months of 1992 alone. Between June 1992 and May 1993, 532 people were killed with AK47s, which were used in bank robberies, theft, and rape, as well as in political rivalry. The police said AK47s could be bought illegally for as little as R100, although one in good condition could fetch up to R2 000. They said the 891 AK47s seized in 1992 were a small proportion of the number of all such weapons in the country. The minister of law and order, Mr Hernus Kriel, said, 'In the beginning the ANC had AK47s. But Inkatha had spears and sticks and stones. So Inkatha started importing arms, and this started an arms race between the organisations to acquire more AK47s. Since then we've witnessed the growth of a web of arms smuggling. It's a major factor in the killings.'[69]

Strategies of the 1980s and 1990s

The conflict among black people has its origins in strategies that were adopted in the 1980s in efforts to force business, the government, the media, and the international community to pay attention to the aspirations of people who had no parliamentary franchise. Their prospects of getting one did not seem very good either, because the government was then still committed to the policy of removing the citizenship of all Africans and hiving them off through the homelands into a separate constitutional orbit. In accordance with this policy, Africans were excluded from the tricameral parliament whose establishment was put to white voters for their approval in a referendum in November 1983. The Institute warned white voters against the exclusion of Africans. A month before the referendum, it brought out a special edition of **Race Relations News**. The front-page headline over a statement about the new tricameral constitution by the Institute's then president was 'Schlemmer warns on stability.' In the same issue the then chairman of the Institute's national executive, Mr Ernie Wentzel, wrote an article on the new constitution headed 'A prescription for creating conflict.'[70]

The Institute warned not only of the consequences of government policies, but also of the consequences of some of the strategies employed in opposition to those policies from 1983 onwards. It in fact warned of the build-up of conflict within the black community from the start. It noted that the use of coercion and of strategies to make the country ungovernable was causing massive disruption to the lives of 'ordinary township residents'.[71] At the same time, however, the Institute urged the government to extend the range of democratic choices open to black people by lifting the bans on the ANC, the Pan-Africanist Congress (PAC), and other organisations to enable them to enter the 'political market-place'. In a paper by the present writer published in November 1984, the Institute also said political prisoners should be released and political exiles allowed to return home, subject to their renunciation of violence. The paper, **Towards a Climate for Negotiation**, said:

> 'No legitimate and lasting solution to South Africa's problems can be found outside structural political change or without some sort of national constitutional conference or equivalent process. Sooner or later the pressure for such a conference will no longer be avoidable. As a first step towards the negotiation on which structural political change must be based, democratic political opportunities within the country need to be widened. Revoking the bannings on political organisations created by black people is the single most effective step that can be taken to initiate this process.'[72]

The Institute's warnings, if anything, were understatements. The government finally broke with its earlier policies on 2nd February 1990, but the resistance strategies adopted in the 1980s continued into 1990, 1991, 1992, and 1993.

Boycotts and stayaways

Consumer, rent, and school boycotts were prominent among these strategies, along with political stayaways from work. Unlike in Soweto in 1976, when strong-arm tactics by militant youths were also used but subsequently repudiated, coercion to enforce compliance with the wishes of political activists was not only widespread in the 1980s and into the 1990s but also a regular feature of the political boycotts and stayaways almost from the moment they began. General 'work stayaways' were sometimes enforced by youths manning barricades, digging up streets, and attacking buses and taxis.[73]

Within a month of the outbreak of violence in September 1984, reports began to come in of schoolchildren being ordered out of class by members of the United Democratic Front (UDF) and the Congress of South African Students, of gangs of youths building barricades in the townships to stop people from going to work, and of activists throwing petrol bombs at the police. At a meeting on 29th October 1984 called by the UDF at the Regina Mundi church in Soweto, one speaker told schoolchildren who wrote matric that they might have police protection while doing so, but there would be no police protection when they went home afterwards.[74] On 4th November 1984 *Sowetan Sunday Mirror* ran an editorial expressing the fear that a stayaway planned for the following two days would, like the previous one, be enforced by coercion and lead, in the newspaper's phrase, to black-on-black violence. People were being dragged 'screaming into the struggle', the newspaper wrote. After the stayaway 16 black consciousness groups met to discuss the problem of coercion. Leaders of the Azanian People's Organisation (Azapo) said that the stayaway had alienated and antagonised a sizeable part of the working class. The Inkatha Freedom Party (IFP) also criticised the stayaway on the grounds that the organisers had employed intimidation and violence against blacks.[75]

The mid 1980s in fact saw well-nigh desperation among black leaders about conflict within black society. Although there was some mention of covert right-wing forces, leader writers on black newspapers and black opinion-makers seemed to believe that the main problem was intolerance and political rivalry within the black community. 'The stoning and burning of people is becoming almost fashionable among blacks', said an editorial in the *Sowetan* on 12th April 1985.[76]

Various liberal groups were aware of all this and even held meetings to discuss it. In the end they decided, in effect, to turn a blind eye to these danger signals nine years ago. The thrust of the meetings was instead to blame the police for all the violence.[77] Thus were sown the seeds of the 'third force' theory.

The flavour of the coercion used to enforce boycotts and stayaways emerges from these few examples:

- four men between the ages of 34 and 63 were hauled in front of a 'people's court' at three o'clock one morning in Soweto after ignoring a stayaway call which they had been told was optional. They were sentenced to 500 lashes each, stripped naked in front of ten-year-olds, spreadeagled over a drum, and flogged. Some people who did not support the stayaway had their ears cut off;
- a man in the Orange Free State was forced to swallow a bottle of tablets he had bought from a pharmacy during a consumer boycott. He died of the overdose;[78]
- in one township, a mother who bought material for her daughter's wedding dress during a consumer boycott was forced to cut it into little pieces; and
- for allegedly breaking a consumer boycott a young mother in the eastern Cape was stabbed at a bus shelter and her baby flung to the ground.[79]

Incidents such as these appear to be the tip of an iceberg. A public opinion survey commissioned by the Institute in 1991 showed that a third of black adults in urban areas answered 'yes' to the question: 'Have you in the past year been forced to take part in a consumer boycott or a stayaway?' At first sight, a third may not seem a large number, but it translates into hundreds of thousands of people and is indeed a high figure given the repeated claim that boycotts and stayaways are voluntary. Two thirds of urban black people claiming to support Azapo or the IFP or even the National Party (NP) said that threats had been used against them, their families or property, to stop them paying rent or service charges or for electricity. Four out of every five people who support Azapo or the IFP claimed to have been forced to take part in boycotts and stayaways.[80]

This coercion, and resistance to it, both extending over several years, may be part of the reason for conflict between supporters of these organisations and supporters of organisations calling for boycotts and stayaways. It may also be part of the reason why hostel residents have become involved in violence, a point to which we will return below.

In this climate of coercion it is impossible to determine how much real support there is for boycotts and stayaways. One of the largest stayaways was an anti-VAT stayaway of 4th and 5th November 1991. It was claimed that 3,5m workers – a quarter of the total economically active population of the country – voluntarily supported it. The claim is partly contradicted by some of the instructions issued. Schoolchildren were thus said to be 'exempt' from the stayaway and told to wear school uniform or carry timetables for identification purposes. Why they should need exemption from action that was said to be voluntary was not explained. Teachers were told to request letters from their headmasters, but the purpose of the letters was not explained. Nor was it stated to whom they had to be shown or why. Committees organising the stayaway apparently agreed that doctors and nurses could go about their normal duties for its duration.[81] Again, the need for the agreement of these committees was not explained.

Any one of a number of reasons could explain why so many people were absent from work on this and other occasions, among them:

- genuine support for the anti-VAT campaign;
- intimidation occurring during the stayaway;
- fear resulting from threats to lives and property shortly before the stayaway;
- experience or knowledge of past coercion; and
- lack of transport (itself possibly the result of fear).

Lack of transport was apparently one of the reasons why so many people were absent from work during a stayaway on 3rd and 4th August 1992.[82] It is probable that many owners and/or drivers of black minibus taxis were themselves sympathetic to the stayaway. It is also possible that many stopped their services because of fear. In some cases intimidation is obvious – burning barricades across roads, for example. But there are other, easier, less obvious ways of ensuring compliance. For example, a stayaway enforcer needs only to stroll casually past a taxi driver and show him a box of matches. The driver's imagination and his memory of necklace executions in newspaper photographs or even on television will do the rest. He will also undoubtedly tell his colleagues and friends about the threat – and so help the process of intimidation, unnoticed by the media or even trained United Nations observers.[83]

Another example of how coercion used over a long period can inculcate feelings of fear appears in bond boycotts launched in apparent protest against high interest rates charged by financial institutions on home loans. These boycotts have frightened off some of the banks and building societies by putting the security of their investments at risk, so helping to slow down the rate of housing construction in black townships. To discourage repossession and resale of houses in respect of which mortgage bond repayments have fallen behind, tyres have sometimes been placed upon the roofs of these houses, with the result that no new occupants dare move in, for the tyres represent an unmistakable threat to any would-be new householder.[84]

Like the example of the box of matches shown to the taxi driver, this highlights what may be a very important aspect of intimidation. It does not need actual threatening behaviour or even threatening words, but merely the quiet display of recognised symbols. Hundreds of black people have been necklaced to death on suspicion of being 'collaborators', 'sellouts', 'informers', and the like, sometimes by frenzied mobs, sometimes on the sentence of self-styled 'people's courts' – for, while the government has stopped executing people, political activists have not. Use of the necklace dropped dramatically after a nation-wide state of emergency was declared in June 1986, only to increase again in 1990 and yet again in 1992.[85] It has replaced the gallows as South Africa's main deterrent.

The initial investment in terror pays off, because people learn to behave in ways expected of them. Knowledge within the community of what happened in the past is sufficient to ensure compliance in the present, and all that is required is a gentle reminder. The quintessence of terror thus involves no violence at all.

In some places localised reigns of terror may keep people permanently cowed. Hostel residents, however, have the advantage that they can use their hostels to mobilise resistance. Professor Lawrence Schlemmer has observed that township residents opposed to mass action would be 'too cautious or fearful to resist'. He adds: 'Migrant workers living in cohesive, socially separated groups, however, are not exposed to the same constraints. Among them mass action will lead to counter-reaction.'[86]

Campaigns against black local authorities

Although the outbreak of violence in Sebokeng in September 1984 occurred during a protest against rent increases, rent and service-charge boycotts have long been more than protests by poor communities against increased tariffs. When increases were suspended in Vaal Triangle townships in 1984, the Vaal Civic Association declared, 'The scrapping of the rent increases is not enough to defuse the situation. Unrest will flare up again unless the council resigns.'[87] Rent boycotts were indeed part of a campaign against black local authorities (BLAs) spearheaded by civic associations affiliated to the UDF. Initially, in 1983, campaigns against BLAs were a reflection of black anger at being fobbed off with local, rather than parliamentary, representation. They took root amid poor living conditions in the country's black townships and included protest against these conditions. The campaigns were, however, also part of an overall strategy to achieve the collapse of apartheid by rendering black areas ungovernable — a strategy pursued by the UDF since its formation in 1983. In 1990 the campaigns were stepped up, despite moves towards national negotiations and non-racial local government.[88]

Black local authorities have long been a source of controversy. Some groups believed in using the various township authorities as a means of improving the lot of township dwellers. Others contended that apartheid could be opposed effectively only by refusing to participate in any of its structures. Like homeland administrations, members of BLAs were seen by many people as 'puppets' and 'collaborators'. As it turned out, BLAs on the whole were ineffective in opposition to apartheid. Many of them were inefficient, even corrupt, and unpopular. However, whereas in 1976/77 the Soweto Urban Bantu Council had been a target of ridicule,[89] now ridicule was replaced by petrol bombs.

Black local authority elections in November and December 1983 were accompanied by coercion on both sides. Householders claimed that councillors tried to secure their votes by threatening to evict them from their houses if they did not comply, while the government claimed there had been 'considerable intimidation' to keep people away from the polls. In Soweto and Port Elizabeth the homes of councillors and/or election candidates were petrol-bombed. From 1984 to the present, black councillors have repeatedly been among the victims of intimidation and violence.

For example, between January 1990 and February 1991 there were at least 195 attacks on black councillors. Sixteen councillors were killed in the 18 months between January 1990 and June 1991. Between August 1990 and February 1991, altogether 358 councillors resigned, 85% saying they had been intimidated into doing so.[90]

The first identified victim of a necklace execution is thought to have been Mr Tamsanqa Kinikini, a member of the black town council in the township of KwaNobuhle in the eastern Cape outside Uitenhage. He had evidently become a hated figure among some of the people there because he was believed to have been involved in corruption and violence.[91] He was hacked and burnt to death a day or two after the police had shot dead some 20 people on 21st March 1985 during a protest march.[92] In addition to Mr Kinikini, three of his sons, aged 13, 20, and 22, his nephew aged 18, and a 20-year-old friend were attacked and killed. Before he died, Mr Kinikini shot another son to prevent his also being hacked to death.[93]

Newspapers said of the killings that they were 'becoming the standard form of punishment meted out to residents believed to be "working for the system"'. Two men, one aged 21 and the other 24, were hanged in September 1987 after being found guilty of the Kinikini murders.[94] During the trial it was stated that a mob had set fire to a mutilated corpse so that a television crew could film them. The court was told that the mob danced around the flaming body chanting and grinning and poking it with sticks while the television camera rolled. One of the accused said in evidence that the television crew had arrived after one of the victims had been killed and burnt, so the body was then doused with petrol and set alight and this action was filmed by the camera crew.[95]

By May 1992, seven years after the Kinikini killings, necklace executions had claimed more than 500 victims. One of those necklaced that month was Mr Esau Mahlatsi, former mayor of Lekoa, which includes the township of Sebokeng, where violence first erupted in September 1984.[96]

The campaign to destabilise black local government has been successful. It has also bred a violent backlash and helped to bring the IFP into urban conflict, because many councillors joined the IFP in the belief that it could protect them. In February 1991, the *Sowetan* reported that jubilant IFP supporters welcomed councillors with 'gunshot' salutes at a rally of some 35 000 people, some of them 'heavily armed with an assortment of traditional weapons', addressed by Chief Mangosuthu Buthelezi in Soweto. The newspaper said that Chief Buthelezi had assured the councillors of support – 'something they have been yearning for for some time'. The following month a senior provincial official with IFP links said, 'It has taken a long time, but now the message is clear. If the ANC carries on with its campaign it will meet organised resistance.' An IFP official, Mr Musa Myeni, said that if councillors joined the organisation 'members of Inkatha in their area will not fold their arms when they are attacked'. Mr Chris Hani later told the South African Institute of Race Relations:

> 'We moved out to attack the institutions of white minority rule... During this phase many councillors were killed... Inkatha moved in by [recruiting] councillors. An attack on councillors came to be seen as an attack on Inkatha.'[97]

Campaigns against policemen

In September 1984 the ANC declared that 'we [ie black South Africans] must be impossible to control'.[98] A Radio Freedom broadcast by the ANC from Addis Ababa on 6th September 1985 bore the headline 'Let the people's war engulf the entire country.' It said that 'police and soldiers must be killed even when they are at their homes, and irrespective of whether they are in uniform or not'.[99] The following month the then president of the ANC, Mr Oliver Tambo, was reported as having said that the intensification of the fight against apartheid would inevitably involve further violence against black councillors and policemen.[100]

Although most of the policemen who have been killed and injured since 1983 were black municipal policemen, all members of the police force, black and white, including policemen in the homelands, have been targets of attack.[101] The South African Police's record of assault on political detainees and criminal suspects, of unprovoked shootings and other aggression, is well documented, notably by the Institute. The poor reputation of the police helped to obscure the emergence of this new aspect of political violence – the attacks on the police. During campaigns of popular mobilisation, violent confrontation has been sparked off sometimes by the police, sometimes by others.[102] Police have also been attacked while off duty and their homes have been petrol-bombed.

The killing of policemen, with their record of violence and aggression in enforcing racial laws and suppressing dissent, would be seen by many as a form of 'just war'. It is necessary, however, to point to the consequences of such a notion. One of them is the very breakdown of order which the government is now expected to restore – even though there has been a steady increase in the number of policemen killed. In 1987 the number of policemen killed was 67, but in 1992 altogether 226 policemen were killed, 96 of them in political violence. By the end of the fourth week in May 1993 another 81 had been killed, bringing the total since July 1983 to 953. According to the minister of law and order, Mr Hernus Kriel, policemen were killed at the rate of one a month in the 1970s, two a month in the 1980s, 13 a month in 1991, and 19 a month in 1992.

In March 1993, Mr Hani told the Institute that 'many policemen' had been killed when 'we moved out to attack the institutions of white minority rule'. However, after the 'stopping of armed struggle...we have appealed to people to stop killing the police'. Also in March 1993, it was reported that the Goldstone Commission had found involvement by the Azanian People's Liberation Army (Apla), military wing of the PAC, in at least 15 attacks on policemen. The police deaths thus cannot all be blamed upon any one organisation or the strategy of making the country ungovernable, especially at a time when Apla was saying 'the South African Police and the security forces are still our targets and we are hitting them at will'. It is nevertheless reasonable to conclude that the revolutionary thrust of earlier years and the impetus of earlier calls for the assassination of policemen and of councillors had not run out.[103]

People's war

In May 1985 Mr Thabo Mbeki, a senior ANC official and now head of the organisation's international affairs function, urged on Radio Freedom that the enemy must be attacked on all fronts, and underground units spread to every factory, mine and farm, every school, and every village. Referring to 'the enemy,' he said: 'We will reply to its reactionary violence with revolutionary violence.'[104] Later that month Mr Tambo broadcast a call on 'our people in the bantustans to isolate and destroy the Pretoria puppets'.[105]

The report of the ANC's commission on strategy and tactics at the organisation's national consultative conference in Kabwe (Zambia) in June 1985 – attended by delegates from both inside and outside South Africa[106] – said that the homelands should clearly 'also be the targets of our movement's efforts to render South Africa ungovernable'. Their governments should be overthrown with a view to 'transforming these areas into bases for the advancement of people's war'.[107]

A great many of the 250 delegates at the Kabwe conference were from the post 1976 generation, and the conference decided to authorise Umkhonto we Sizwe to strike at 'soft' (civilian) targets as well as to intensify 'people's war'.[108] Later in 1985 Mr Tambo told the foreign affairs committee of the British House of Commons that 'We are reaching a level of conflict where the innocent are hit. It is unavoidable. Now there is going to be more bloodshed than ever before.'[109]

The people's war was seen as all-embracing. A Radio Freedom broadcast in December 1986 urged that the masses should fight 'in every way possible using...Molotov cocktails, spears, sticks, petrol bombs, and small arms seized from whites'. Other forms of struggle should also be used: 'We are talking about rent strikes, we are talking about bus boycotts, we are talking about the overthrow of the township councils of the puppets and the creation of people's organs of power, people's courts and so on. All these various elements of the struggle help to make up the total aggregate of a people's war.'[110]

To what extent were broadcasts and policy decisions translated into action? In June 1985 it was reported that about 80 attacks by Umkhonto we Sizwe since the Nkomati Accord showed that the ANC had demonstrated its capacity to maintain an armed presence in South Africa without bases in neighbouring states. Simple military training was being provided within the country, the speed of reaction to internal political events showing the extent to which internal guerrillas operated on their own initiative.[111] An ANC official was quoted at the end of the year as saying that 'our guerrilla presence inside South Africa is organic in that our fighters are self-sustaining'.[112]

At the end of 1986 the ANC was claiming that about 50 trained Umkhonto guerrillas were returning to South Africa every month, while 'well-placed sources in the front-line states' said that about 500 fully trained ANC men were operational in South Africa, mainly in training roles, providing skills and guidance to young black militants.[113]

In a speech in London, Mr Joe Slovo, who preceded Mr Hani as general secretary of the SACP and chief of staff of Umkhonto we Sizwe and is now national chairman of the SACP and a senior office-bearer in the ANC, said that 'mass political struggle, coupled with an intensification of revolutionary violence, remains the imperative'.[114] A journalist who later disclosed that he had been working clandestinely for the ANC[115] wrote that the 'revolutionary forces' of which the ANC spoke 'comprised not only itself, the SACP, and the South African Congress of Trade Unions, but also a large number of other organisations inside the country'.[116] Mr Tambo said that the ANC would have to have its own 'underground structures within the UDF' to give it 'the correct guidance'.[117]

The 'people's war' involved mobilising youth – described by Mr Tambo as 'young lions'[118] – and bringing education to a standstill. Black youths have remained politically fired up since the Soweto revolt against Bantu education in particular and apartheid in general. Determined that they will not live out their lives under the system of apartheid in the way that so many of their parents did, black youth are not only prepared to die for the struggle, as hundreds if not thousands have done, some are also prepared to kill for it.

The rate of growth of the South African economy – an annual average of some 6% during the 1960s – halved in the 1970s and halved again in the 1980s. By the end of that decade, only about 125 of the 1 000 young people joining the labour market each day were finding jobs in the formal sector of the economy. There was accordingly no shortage of frustrated youngsters willing to be mobilised.[119]

In a broadcast on 12th September 1986 Mr Hani praised the youth for 'carrying out aspects of the people's war' by 'clearing our townships of collaborators' and 'puppets and agents of the regime'. Another broadcast that month hailed the closure of more than 20 black schools in the Transvaal and the eastern Cape as 'another defeat' for the 'enemy'. The broadcast said: 'If need be, let Botha close all black schools in the country.'[120] Necklace victims included black schoolboys who wrote their matric exams in apparent defiance of boycotts.[121]

In an editorial in 1990 the black Sunday newspaper *City Press* blamed 'the youth in our society' for their 'political immaturity' in introducing 'the necklace method of killing' and going on the 'rampage, stoning and burning houses belonging to rival activists'.[122]

The youth may indeed have done all this for nearly a decade, but they were encouraged to do it by adults. In 1986, for example, the *Sunday Times* of London reported that the then general secretary of the ANC, Mr Alfred Nzo, had said that 'collaborators with the enemy' must be eliminated. The paper went on: 'Asked if this included necklacing, Nzo nodded emphatically. "Whatever the people decide to use to eliminate those enemy elements is their decision. If they decide to use necklacing, we support it".'[123]

In an article in which he refers to necklace killings and to fear of 'comrades' in the townships, Mr Joe Latakgomo, former editor of the *Sowetan* and later senior assistant editor of *The Star*, wrote: 'The earlier mobilisation of our youth against "collaborators" spawned this culture, which will take generations to eliminate.'[124]

In July 1989, six months before Mr Mandela was released from prison, a meeting of the ANC, the UDF, and the Congress of South African Trade Unions (Cosatu) in Lusaka decided to promote an 'upsurge' of 'volcanic material' and ensure 'that our programme of action is capable of firing up the imagination of the people and building up action to increasingly higher levels'.[125]

Political violence as measured by monthly fatalities had been in double digits for most of 1987 and 1988 and for all but one month in the first half of 1989. In August that year monthly fatalities entered triple digits and by the end of May 1993, more than three and a half years later, had not once dropped to double figures again. In December 1989, the number of political fatalities climbed to nearly 300, for the first time ever. This sustained upsurge in violence may be partly the result of decisions taken in Lusaka.

At the end of 1989 a 'conference for a democratic future' held at the University of the Witwatersrand decided to intensify the struggle against homeland administrations and black local authorities.[126] In March and April 1990 various newspapers announced the collapse of the homelands as violence flared in Bophuthatswana, Gazankulu, Lebowa, Venda, and the Ciskei. The numbers of fatalities in the four constitutionally separate homelands (the Transkei, Bophuthatswana, Venda, and the Ciskei) increased from zero in the first three months of 1989 to 53 in the first three months of 1990.[127] In January 1991 the ANC said that it would hit Bophuthatswana hard. Campaigns to destabilise Bophuthatswana and the Ciskei were launched in 1991 and 1992.[128]

Consequences of people's war

These coercive strategies, intensified struggles, assassination campaigns, mass actions, and volcanic upsurges of fired-up people have had two consequences. The one is that they have got out of control. As Mr Mandela said in March 1992, it is difficult to make young ANC members understand a need for change after they had been 'told to make the country ungovernable'.[129] The campaign to make South Africa ungovernable may not have succeeded universally and it may or may not have been subsequently abandoned, but it has succeeded beyond expectation in some parts of the country.

The other consequence of these strategies is that they have provoked violent backlashes from at least some of their targets and set off a vicious circle of attack and counter-attack. In boycotts and stayaways black people were incidental victims of violence; in the ungovernability strategy they were high on the list of intended targets. The people's war was partly directed at the state but it was also a declaration of war against sections of the black community, some of whom, however, fought back.

The shift from 'armed struggle' to 'people's war' was of crucial importance. As Mr Tambo explained, the people's war involved the masses 'rather than an army with guerrillas' in 'popular revolutionary action'. There was some doubt at the time within the ANC as to whether the ANC 'had the local organisational resources to remain in control of the forces it would unleash'.[130] Sending trained squads of insurgents to plant limpet mines or car bombs is one thing. Urging the masses as a whole, and angry youth in particular, to a no-holds-barred people's war is quite another – especially when, as an ANC office-bearer subsequently said with reference to the post 1976 recruits, they were less disciplined than earlier ones and 'the only thing they wanted was to carry a gun'.[131] Disciplined violence is replaced by random violence. Indeed, where armed struggle implies command structures (which can, and indeed, did suspend the armed struggle in the agreement between the ANC and the government recorded in the Pretoria Minute of 6th August 1990), people's war unleashes forces which have no command structures to control them or curtail them. In terms of casualties, the armed struggle of the 1960s and 1970s and early 1980s was a minor affair compared with the violence unleashed by the people's war of the mid 1980s. Thus, in the nine years up to the end of 1985, an annual average of 18 people (including civilians, security personnel, and insurgents) were killed in the 'armed struggle', whereas fatalities on all sides since January 1985 are running at an annual average in excess of 1 850 – more than 100 times the rate in 'armed struggle'.[132]

Paradoxically, however, the people's war attracted less attention and criticism. The killing of innocent civilians by limpet mines in such places as shopping centres in white areas[133] generated massive and usually adverse publicity. By contrast, Institute research shows that on many occasions attacks on black councillors attracted no press attention at all, still less criticism, even though the victims were sometimes their wives or children.[134] Because most of its targets were black, the people's war could be waged almost unnoticed by the white community.

After political fatalities soared in March 1990 to above both 300 and 400 for the first time ever, the Institute predicted that if violence continued at its higher levels the year would be the most violent in the country's history.[135] Just as the Institute's warnings of the build-up of tension in Soweto schools prior to the explosion on 16th June 1976 proved correct (although they fell on deaf ears)[136] the fear about 1990 was right – 3 699 people died. At the time, however, rightly or wrongly the Institute suspected that the government tried sometimes to play down the political violence and to dismiss the revolutionary language sometimes used by political leaders as 'rhetoric'.[137] The Institute had the impression, admittedly subjective, that at least some sections of the white population did not want to confront the problem of worsening violence for fear of damping the euphoria in the first few months after Mr de Klerk's speech of 2nd February.[138]

When the ANC agreed in August that year to suspend armed struggle, there was speculation in the press that the government wanted the organisation to go further. Although apparently no government spokesman said so in as many words, several different newspapers reported government sources as wanting the ANC also to suspend mass mobilisation, which the government was said to regard as 'disguised violence'.[139]

After the talks, the ANC said in an advertisement that suspending the armed struggle meant that the organisation 'will not carry out any further armed actions and related activities such as the infiltration of armed cadres and weaponry'. The advertisement added that the 'armed struggle has not been abandoned' and that 'Umkhonto we Sizwe has not been dissolved.' Under a heading 'mass action continues' it said 'mass struggles have to continue in all spheres of our lives to achieve our objective of a united non-racial democratic and non-sexist society'.[140]

When the government imposed a localised state of emergency in 1985 and a nationwide emergency in 1986, it did so less because of armed struggle launched from neighbouring states than because of internal mass mobilisation by the still-banned ANC and its internal allies in the UDF. As the ANC made clear in the advertisements, however, it did not regard the lifting of the banning order on itself on 2nd February 1990 as a reason to abandon mass action strategies. Had it done so, it might have alienated some of its supporters, notably among the youth, especially those without jobs or much prospect of finding them, because of lack of education, or low economic growth, or racial discrimination on the part of employers, or all three.

Mass action continued into 1991, 1992, and 1993. The ANC's consultative conference in December 1990 resolved that the following year would be 'the year of mass action for the transfer of power to the people'. In November 1991 mass action culminated in the deaths of about 100 people in the anti-VAT stayaway. Opening the ANC's policy conference in May the following year, Mr Mandela said negotiations would in future be coupled with mass action as a 'deadlock-breaking mechanism' and to compel the government to transfer power to the people. Speaking at the funeral on 29th June 1992 of 37 victims of the Boipatong massacre, Mr Hani warned that mass action would involve a 'fight to the finish...until we defeat De Klerk'.

At about the same time, after the Convention for a Democratic South Africa reached deadlock, the ANC/SACP/Cosatu alliance launched a programme of 'rolling' mass action designed to bring about the downfall of the government. In the words of one official,

> 'What we are talking about now is a spiral, of building up our forces from about a million in the build-up phase to the active involvement of 10 million in phase 4. We are looking at the possibility of the Leipzig option. The decision is that we now utilise mass action until we reach the stage where De Klerk is propelled out of the exit gate.'

In July the same year Mr Mandela was reported as having said that the people of Africa would make Iran's Islamic revolution a model for their own revolutionary action.[141]

The ANC condemned necklacing in 1992 and also stated that the killing of policemen would play into the hands of the right wing,[142] while Mr Mandela stated that the objective of the renewed mass action campaign launched that year was not insurrection.[143] But at the time of writing it was not clear whether the people's war against collaborators or the campaign against black local authorities and certain homelands had been called off. A prominent ANC leader in Natal, Mr Harry Gwala, said in August 1992 that mass action should be intensified with a view to making the country more ungovernable than it was in the state of emergency years.[144] Even before the march on Bisho, capital of the Ciskei, on 7th September 1992, which culminated in the killing of 28 ANC supporters by Ciskei security forces – who were subsequently indemnified against prosecution – some ANC officials said the organisation would continue to make the Ciskei ungovernable. The national executive committee of the ANC had indeed published a document endorsing proposals for the intensification of mass action, focused, inter alia, on Bophuthatswana, the Ciskei, KwaZulu, and QwaQwa.[145] Subsequent to the Bisho shootings the general secretary of the ANC, Mr Cyril Ramaphosa, said: 'We are determined to cleanse this country. After Gqozo we are going for you Mangope; after Mangope we are going for you Buthelezi.'[146]

The cycle of attack and counter-attack

The murderous cycle of attack and counter-attack to which reference has already been made dates back to August 1976 in Soweto, to the clashes between residents of the Mzimhlope hostel and township youths during a stayaway. These clashes have sometimes been poorly reported. A group called the Independent Board of Inquiry issued a booklet which said that the issue on that occasion was 'what hostel-dwellers described as their right to refuse to participate in a work stayaway'. On the day of the stayaway, the booklet says, 'youths taunted the men on their way to work' while in the 'evening, when the hostel residents disembarked from Mzimhlope station, they had to run the gauntlet of residents'. By the time the men reached the hostel, three sons of a resident were dead and by the next morning 48 people, mostly residents, were dead. In evidence submitted to the

Cillie Commission, the Institute described how the hostel residents had gone on the rampage after students had set fire to their hostel.[147] The commission found that youths had spread a rumour among the hostel residents that some of their fellow hostellers were being assaulted at the station on their way back from work (which had happened on a previous occasion).[148] When the one group of hostellers rushed to their colleagues' assistance, the hostel was set on fire. When the hostellers returned they attacked the youths, allegedly with police encouragement. A hostel resident was sprinkled with petrol, which was ignited.[149] All of this the booklet reduces to a 'taunt'. Peace was restored in this area by the end of 1976, but ten years later conflict between residents of this hostel and their neighbours broke out again. It continued into the 1990s.[150]

Conflict also erupted between militant youth and hostel residents in Cape Town at the end of 1976. Some of the youngsters raided a shebeen in one of the hostels in the Nyanga township. Hostel residents retaliated, storming into the streets, burning houses, and attacking people with spears, knives, knobkerries, rocks, iron bars, axes, and other weapons. Five thousand people fled Nyanga to seek sanctuary in other townships and in white suburbs. Eighty-one houses were destroyed and 94 extensively damaged when hostellers set them on fire. In reprisal, five hostel buildings were burnt down. More than a hundred people were seriously injured, and a police witness later told the Cillie Commission that 13 black people had been shot dead by the police in these December clashes, while 23 had died when black people fought each other. Some township residents said the number of deaths would have been higher had the police not intervened. Others accused the police of preventing householders from defending their homes against the hostellers and of assisting the hostellers to attack.[151]

The incidents in 1976 were harbingers of things to come: a backlash by hostel residents against militant youth; retaliation out of all proportion to the scale of attack; allegations of police involvement on one side; and the momentum which the cycle of attack and counter-attack appears to have developed.

The fighting does not necessarily take a party-political form. Attackers and counter-attackers may not be supporters of political organisations, and even if they are, they may not be under the control of leaders of these organisations. The backlash against coercion may sometimes be a manifestation of ordinary people acting violently in a pre-emptive, retaliatory, or aggressive fashion.

For example, in 1985 it was reported that three pupils at a secondary school in Soweto had been kidnapped and beaten by a group of more than 100 'Russians' (tribesmen) in revenge for a raid on them by students who assaulted a man they suspected of stabbing a colleague. The *Sowetan* reported, 'This is the first time residents have taken action against continuing raids on them by students in Soweto.'[152] It was also reported that members of the Zion Christian Church (ZCC) had gone on the 'rampage' armed with weapons ranging from sjamboks to pangas searching houses in Alexandra township. They were evidently retaliating for attacks on some of their members by youths who had confiscated their church badges and in some cases forced them to chew these badges because the ZCC had invited State President P W Botha to address them at the church's headquarters at Moria in the northern Transvaal over the preceding Easter weekend.[153] An Orlando resident wrote to the *Sunday Times* in a letter published in August 1985 that men on buses stoned by youths were scared of fighting back because something terrible might happen to their families. However, they were now vowing to fight back.[154] In 1987 it was reported that UDF members had been attacked by 'vigilantes' in KwaNobuhle who were 'tired of the intimidation of comrades holding the township to ransom'.[155] In July 1986 the Institute suggested that the growth of vigilantes was possibly a reaction to coercive strategies used by revolutionaries.[156]

One of the most recent violent backlashes against coercion occurred during the anti-VAT stayaway at the President Steyn gold mine in November 1991. In reporting the violence, *The Star* ran a headline 'Claims of third force behind President Steyn violence' on its front page. The Goldstone Commission found no evidence to substantiate these allegations. The Commission found instead that two initial killings by stayaway enforcers led to revenge attacks, counter-attacks, ethnic conflict, and involvement of a gang of 'Russians' from a neighbouring township, at the end of which 86 people were dead and 403 injured.[157]

Although violence is not always party-political, it is apparent that the ANC and/or the UDF on the one hand and the IFP on the other are involved in major conflict. Four examples of conflict on the Reef in 1991 and 1992 show that both sides were both victims and aggressors, but also that it is often not clear exactly what happened or what the political allegiances of participants were.

On 19th April 1991 Mr Moses Khumalo, mayor of Soweto's Diepmeadow township and chairman of the local IFP branch, was ambushed and shot dead with an AK47. Although there is some doubt as to whether his murder was political the IFP was convinced that it was part of the campaign against black local authorities. There had been at least four previous attempts on his life.[158]

After the funeral on Sunday 27th April, ten people were hacked and stabbed to death, allegedly by IFP members. The IFP claimed that this attack was provoked when a bus carrying funeral-goers was fired at with AK47s from a house in the Meadowlands township. Funeral-goers who chased one of the AK47 attackers killed him in his kitchen. Further attack and counter-attack followed, and by the end of the first week in May, 66 people in Soweto were dead in clashes between the ANC and the IFP.[159] What appears to have happened is that a hit-and-run attack was launched against the funeral-goers, after which the attackers disappeared into the surrounding houses. Their targets chased after them, but unable to find all the actual attackers, took revenge on communities presumed to be sheltering them.

The ANC/IFP conflict has spilled over, particularly on the Reef and south of Johannesburg down to the Vaal River, into violence on trains and between hostel residents and other people. The most notorious example of the latter type of conflict was the massacre apparently launched by IFP supporters from the Boipatong hostel in Sebokeng in June 1992. Some people saw hostels on the Reef as military barracks from which IFP supporters launched attacks. The *Sowetan*, for example, claimed that one hostel – which it described as an 'Inkatha garrison' – in Alexandra township had been the source of attacks that had resulted in nearly 200 deaths.[160] Following the Boipatong massacre, the ANC renewed demands for the fencing of hostels to prevent their being used as bases for attacks on neighbouring communities.[161]

It was, moreover, reported that one of the main problems experienced by the police in their fight against arms smuggling was the virtual impenetrability of hostels. One detective commented: 'You can't just walk in there.' Another said: 'You are faced with thousands of people...and you encounter a great deal of hostility...and if you do go in there, you can forget about friendly co-operation. For instance, we get a tip-off at 3pm that there are 15 AKs in a hostel room – but by the time we get in, the arms are gone, because they knew that we were coming.'[162]

IFP officials said hostel residents were being organised along military lines to 'defend themselves against people who want to demolish the hostels'.[163] Hostel residents were not safe in their dwellings or on the way to work because Umkhonto we Sizwe had sheltered behind the ANC and 'gone crazy'.[164]

The Boipatong massacre was not the first. One earlier example of conflict between hostel residents and others was in May 1991, when 28 people were murdered at the Swanieville squatter settlement near Kagiso on the west Rand. At the time the police said that the attack on the predominantly Xhosa squatters had been launched by 1 000 residents of a mainly Zulu hostel. There were allegations of collusion between the police and the attackers, Mr Mandela dismissing claims that the police had been unaware of what he said were IFP plans for the massacre. The police, he said, had spies in every hostel, and if hostel dwellers 'decide to attack tomorrow, the police will know immediately'. Mr Mandela said the massacres were happening because 'it has become the policy of the government to allow this in order to weaken the liberation movement'. The IFP, he said, wanted 'to rise to power on the corpses of dead people'.[165]

The IFP said that, for more than a week preceding the violence, residents of the hostel had been subjected to repeated intimidation and sporadic attacks, including stonings, stabbings, and shootings, from people living in the squatter camp. The day before the massacre two hostel residents had been abducted and taken into the squatter camp. They had not been seen since and it was not known whether they were dead or alive. A delegation from the hostel had gone to the squatter camp and asked that the abducted men be set free. The squatters apparently refused to free them and threatened the delegation. This was 'the last straw' for hostel residents. Denying prior knowledge of the massacre, the IFP said: 'IFP members in hostels are being constantly targeted for attack and have had enough. They are frightened, angry and defensive.'[166]

In February 1993 following a trial arising from the massacre, a judge said it was a scandal that only seven men had been charged. Acquitting them for lack of evidence, he said the police should have been able, using video cameras, to bring a strong case against at least 100 people instead of a doubtful case against seven.[167]

Later that same year, conflict broke out in Tokoza, south-east of Johannesburg, and then spread to neighbouring communities. According to a report subsequently drawn up by a committee of the Goldstone Commission, peace had prevailed in the area from February 1991 to 8th September 1991, on which day 18 hostel residents were massacred en route to a meeting in a stadium. The Goldstone report said that the hostel residents had been ambushed following arrangements made at a meeting of a 'self-defence unit' (one of whose members was found to be a police informer) based in the nearby Phola Park squatter settlement. The attack had been executed with a 'high degree of professionalism' by small units of three men each located at three (and possibly four) corners of the stadium.

Three weeks later, on 29th September, Mr Sam Ntuli, general secretary of the Civic Association of Southern Transvaal, was assassinated in the same street in which the 18 hostel residents had been murdered. The Goldstone committee said it could not come to any conclusion as to who had killed Mr Ntuli, but it mentioned the fact that the incident occurred three weeks after the assassination of the hostel residents. Described by the *Saturday Star* as 'a man with a mission' who 'aimed to wipe black local authorities off the map', Mr Ntuli had escaped a petrol-bomb attack on his house the preceding February in which two children were injured. He blamed the IFP for the attack.[168]

Eight days after his death, on 7th October, which was a normal working Monday, a stayaway was called and mourners performed a hand-washing ceremony at Mr Ntuli's parents' home. After leaving the house some of the funeral-goers took part in an attack on a taxi rank, apparently either because the taxi drivers did not participate in the stayaway or because they were (falsely) believed to be supporters of the IFP. After this attack there was an attack on funeral-goers which led to the deaths of another 18 people. The Goldstone investigation concluded that these murders were premeditated and possibly a retaliation for the earlier assassination of the hostel residents. It said, however, that it did not hear evidence sufficient to conclude that the murders were carried out by or on behalf of hostel residents.

On 26th February 1992 four passengers in a minibus transporting employees of the Rand Water Board from Tokoza were murdered on the Old Vereeniging Road near Phola Park. The committee found that this was a carefully contrived attack, apparently because the owner of the minibus was a member of the IFP. It said that the attack was planned and mounted by the Phola Park 'self-defence unit', which had on 'no occasions during the period in question played a defensive role' and was apparently not under the command of Umkhonto we Sizwe.

On 3rd April, 19 people were killed in what became known as the Crossroads massacre. Crossroads, a squatter settlement north of Tokoza, is occupied mainly by Zulus. On 6th April, four people were killed in an attack on Zonkizizwe, a squatter settlement further south under the control of the IFP, which, said the Goldstone committee, 'does not permit any other political activity in the area'. The committee said it could not identify the reasons for either of these attacks or the political persuasions of the perpetrators, although it was satisfied that they fell within the pattern of attack, counter-attack, revenge, and reconciliation.[169]

An ANC member subsequently pleaded not guilty to 21 murder charges arising from the attack on the hostel residents on 8th September 1991 and the attack on the minibus.[170] This trial, like that of the 32 IFP supporters charged with the Boipatong killings, was in progress at the time of writing.

In an interim report on train violence published in July 1992, the Goldstone Commission said that whenever a group of attackers was identified they turned out to be hostel dwellers, mainly Zulus, traditionally linked to the IFP. In May 1993 in a further report on train violence – which claimed 216 lives in 1992 alone – the commission said it was clear that attacks emanated from hostels as well as from surrounding townships. There was no foundation for any finding that hostel residents were mainly responsible for the attacks on commuters. The report also said that although train violence arose from ANC/IFP enmity, there was no evidence that either organisation had actively encouraged its perpetration.[171]

To describe the ANC/IFP conflict simply as a power struggle between them begs the question as to why they are fighting. How and when violent conflict between the two organisations actually started requires full investigation,[172] although the first signs of it appear to have been as early as 1977 in Natal and 1986 on the Reef.[173] It would appear that the strategy to make the country ungovernable that was adopted eight or nine years ago, focused in particular at homeland administrations[174] and black local authorities, and the backlash it has provoked, are among the main reasons for the violence that now afflicts South Africa. In 1986 Chief Buthelezi was described as a 'counter-revolutionary' who was playing 'a leading role in organising vigilantes attacking those fighting for liberation'. In November 1986, Radio Freedom said in a broadcast, 'It is clear the puppet Gatsha [Buthelezi] is being groomed by the West and the racist regime to become a Savimbi in a future free South Africa. The onus is on the people of South Africa to neutralise the Gatsha snake, which is poisoning the people of South Africa. It needs to be hit on the head.'[175]

Mr Hani later said that the strategy of rendering the state ungovernable had not been merely a question of 'rhetoric': 'We moved out to attack the institutions of white minority rule – the black local authorities, the collaborationist chiefs, the police both black and white, whom we saw as instruments of oppression.' There was, he said, a 'physical campaign...to wipe out puppets and stooges'. Politically speaking, Chief Buthelezi was an enemy, Mr Hani said. 'Our propaganda on Radio Freedom was very sharp. We called on the people to oppose him. We called him a stooge and a puppet.'

After the ANC had abandoned armed struggle in 1990 but continued mass action, Mr Hani said, the IFP had adopted a strategy of always opposing ANC initiatives, such as stayaways, and boycotts.

The IFP was seen as trying to 'frustrate the liberation movement'. It had 'suddenly became openly aggressive', marching with weapons and red headbands.[176]

According to the Inkatha Institute, part of the ANC/UDF strategy of 'rural mobilisation' in the early 1980s was 'the military empowerment of the youth' in order 'to attack not only government structures (including KwaZulu) but also tribal structures'. The Inkatha Institute claims that the strategy involved the systematic 'elimination of tribal chiefs, mostly Inkatha supporting', and the replacement of tribal courts with 'people's courts'.[177]

Whatever its origins, the ANC/IFP conflict and other conflict in black communities has no doubt been exploited by straight criminal elements, and by reactionary whites, some of whom may be present or past members of security forces. It is nevertheless striking that in fifteen and a half pages of single-spaced transcript of an interview with the Institute, mainly devoted to a discussion of the reasons for conflict between the ANC and the IFP, Mr Hani focused on factors such as the above, mentioning only in passing that a 'third force' was exploiting the animosity between the IFP and the ANC and beginning to make use of elements in the KwaZulu police.

Allegations of right-wing elements provoking conflict among blacks have not been made only in the context of ANC/IFP conflict. In July 1985 the *Sunday Times* reported that 'hideous atrocities' were being committed in the name of the struggle for regional supremacy between the UDF and Azapo in the eastern Cape, but that leaders of both organisations claimed that neither of them had anything to do with the violence. They hinted at the involvement of an ultra right-wing 'third force'. These allegations were made at the same time as Mr Goniwe was murdered. The newspaper said that the murders underscored the endemic violence which had plagued the region for the past 12 months.[178]

When Mr Ntuli was murdered the *Saturday Star* devoted almost an entire page to his death and the campaign against black councillors. It quoted him as describing the councillors as the 'actual source of violence against people', and as claiming that Cast had more than 50 'defence units', but the article did not mention any of the violence directed against councillors.[179]

Press reporting on violence

The omission is a good example of how aspects of violence are under-reported by the media. There appear to be various reasons for this.

Although press censorship by the state all but disappeared during the later years of the 1980s, a new kind of censorship emerged as political activists threatened and sometimes man-handled black reporters. One senior black journalist observed that criticising strategies such as class boycotts was considered taboo by political activists, some of whom organised class boycotts in Soweto but sent their children to private schools in white areas. But if a journalist dared to write about this, he was seen as being 'against the struggle'. The weapon used then 'was to whisper, to spread the word around, that so-and-so is against the struggle'. The journalist added, 'Heaven help you should you ever be cornered by youngsters: they will make you pay for being against the struggle.'

In the mid 1980s, black reporters blamed the ANC and the UDF for most of this intimidation – which received minimal attention in most white newspapers – but added that the PAC, Azapo, and the IFP also threatened journalists.[180]

Another reason why violence is not comprehensively reported could be party-political preferences among journalists. A number of journalists sought in the late 1970s, as one of them put it, to radically 'redefine the agenda of news in South Africa'. Mr Howard Barrell thus wrote in an article in the *New Statesman and Society* in February 1990 that he had 'worked clandestinely' for the ANC for ten years on the 'South African commercial press'. He said that his task 'as a journalist intervening for the ANC in the press' was 'to create as much space as possible for reportage on the ANC'. This work had involved 'years of necessary deception', inter alia of 'morally diffident editors and controllers of the liberal established press'. The reportage did not necessarily have to be favourable. The important point 'was that the [ANC] be reported in sustained fashion on top of the news agenda as being, generally, the racist congregation's anti-Christ'.[181]

Research by the Institute has found that newspapers, including the established commercial press, have played down certain types of violence, in particular violence against black councillors and the police. For example, in a seven-month period that the Institute monitored between January and July 1990, there were more than 400 attacks on councillors and the police, but more than half of them were not reported in any one of the six English-language newspapers published in Johannesburg. There were also relatively few photographs which dealt with attacks on councillors or policemen, yet right-wing violence and intimidation were regularly featured, prominently displayed, and reported on by teams of investigative journalists accompanied by photographers.[182]

Violence in the anti-VAT stayaway was also played down. For example, by Wednesday 6th November some 24 people were already dead in the stayaway, among them 15 killed in the first stage of violence at President Steyn. Yet in its front-page story that day evaluating the stayaway, *The Star* chose to highlight claims that it had been a victory for the National Peace Accord signed on 14th September 1991. The paper's editorial that day quoted the claim by a trade union official that 'there have been fewer deaths in the last two days of peaceful protest than there are during the normal running of the country'. The newspaper seemed to agree with him and to share his complacency. It relegated the fatalities to virtual postscript status at the bottom of the article.[183]

The outrage over the Boipatong massacre contrasted powerfully with the manner in which twice as many deaths in the anti-VAT stayaway were shrugged off by the media. Churches and foreign governments donated money for the Boipatong victims' families and many diplomats and prominent personalities were represented at the funeral. Yet these churches and foreign governments do not seem to have started funds for the families of the 86 anti-VAT victims. There was no national day of mourning for them, nor an international outcry. As far as the present writer is aware, there is no fund for the families of 500 or more victims of necklace executions, nor was there any diplomatic ceremony at their funerals.[184]

Newspapers which had propagated the 'third force' theory to explain violence were taken aback by the findings of the Goldstone Commission at the end of May 1992 that one of the main causes of violence was the political conflict between the ANC and the IFP. Many people had already reached this conclusion themselves, but

The Star described the Goldstone statement as a 'bombshell' and said ANC officials had raised 'serious questions about the future credibility of the government-appointed commission'.

The Weekly Mail ran two long articles attacking Mr Justice Goldstone.[185] He had, the paper said, 'stunned political and legal observers' by putting the blame for violence largely on the conflict between the ANC and the IFP. Why these anonymous 'observers' should be 'stunned' by this statement is not explained. What particularly angered *The Weekly Mail* was Judge Goldstone's statement that he had received 'no evidence' to suggest the existence of a 'third force' in the sense of a sinister and secret organisation orchestrating political violence on a wide front. The paper maintained that the Goldstone finding had given policemen and the state 'new licence', presumably to carry out acts of criminal violence.

The author of the articles denouncing Judge Goldstone was evidently so absorbed in that exercise that he had no time to read some of the other articles that appeared in the same edition of *The Weekly Mail*. On page one the newspaper said,

> 'The revolt of township youths in the Vaal is already uglier that the uprisings of June 1976. Today's youths are armed, their violence anarchic and random, their targets innocent passers-by. A little-publicised state of emergency has been declared in the Vaal area. Streets are barricaded and schooling has stopped... Behind the apparently aimless violence lies a desperate cry for help from a generation whose schooling has been intermittent and inadequate and whose futures look bleak.'

On page four the paper said, 'In the 1980s, targets of resistance were clearly defined: killing councillors and other government officials, petrol bombing houses and company vehicles and defying consumer boycotts were legitimate activities, according to anti-apartheid movements intent on rendering the townships ungovernable.' Another article on the same page says, 'The youths believe in mobs. Being in a mob is safer. The youngest [involved in the fighting] are about 9 years.' On page six there is an article about 'vicious internecine feuds...flaring up around the country between renegade members of Umkhonto we Sizwe and other anti-apartheid veterans'. The murder of a shop steward at Iscor is put down to a squabble between pro-ANC union shop stewards and a local unit of Umkhonto we Sizwe members. Further on in the article reference is made to a township near Durban which is a hot bed of intrigue and tension between resident comrades and Umkhonto members just returned from exile. Later in the article 'open violence between ANC supporters and an MK-led faction in the Phola Park squatter camp' on the East Rand is mentioned. Another article on the same page says that 'mayhem is compounded by factionalism within the ANC's Vaal region, which has degenerated into internal violence'.

On page 12 there is a report about hundreds of students who 'rampaged' across the Durban campus of the University of Natal, 'wrecking buildings and equipment', in protest against the exclusion from the university in March of a student who had failed 16 out of 22 exams in two years. Further on we learn about 'bizarre stories' in which 'students tell of the GTIs and the "thugmobile" who allegedly drag students from their rooms to join protest action'. GTI, the article says, stands for 'get them intimidated'. In attempting to explain why there is so much 'distrust, racial tension and conflict' on the campus, the article says, 'Some blame the "ungovernability" heritage of 1980s student behaviour. "Then anything was excusable", said one student leader. "You could rape someone to get information and get away with it".'

In seeking to discredit the Goldstone Commission for blaming violence on the ANC and the IFP instead of only on the IFP or on a 'third force', *The Weekly Mail* was ignoring the facts about ungovernability and anarchy and all the other causes of the violence that were at last beginning to be reported in its columns. The paper accused Judge Goldstone of being 'ahistorical' yet the newspaper itself appeared to have forgotten all about strategies of 'liberation before education' that helped to bring about the unending tragedy of township youngsters who were once romanticised as 'young lions' but who are now the despair of the country – so much so that Mr Hani, shortly before his death almost a year later, was talking about transforming township 'self-defence units' into a type of 'peace corps' in order to regain control over them.[186]

The legitimation of revolutionary violence

Violence in South Africa may have got out of control. But it did so in a situation where the use of violence for political purposes was seen by many as legitimate and morally acceptable in the name of a 'just war'.

Violence does not occur in a vacuum. It draws oxygen from public opinion which supports it or condones it. The violence of pass arrests and forced population removals, along with the violence inflicted on black detainees in police cells, and on black demonstrators on the streets, was endorsed by white voters in South Africa as the National Party won election after election. These policies were also for many years endorsed by the Afrikaner establishment, including the churches, many intellectuals, and the Afrikaans-controlled media. There are many reasons why the NP abandoned these policies. One of them is the withdrawal of intellectual, press, and church endorsement.

These considerations also apply at the other end of the spectrum.

Churches

The just war against the enemy and his collaborators has explicit ecclesiastical blessing, even though some South African church leaders deny this.[187] The fact that churches may also have preached or tried to play a role in reconciliation does not alter this fact. It only confuses the moral message – as is evident from a statement in 1991 by the ANC Youth League, which spoke of the 'courageous efforts the men of the cloth have made to achieve peace' but also said that the church had advocated the use of organised violence.[188]

The role played by some South African churches in creating a climate in which people feel they could use violence, free of moral restraint, has probably been greatly underestimated.

In May 1987, the World Council of Churches' Programme to Combat Racism held a conference in Lusaka, the South African delegation to which included 30 church leaders chosen by the South African Council of Churches (SACC). The meeting issued a statement which included the following: 'While remaining committed to peaceful liberation we recognise that the nature of the South African regime which wages war against its own inhabitants and neighbours compels the [liberation] movements to the use of force along with other means to end oppression.' At the same time, the churches gathered in Lusaka condemned the mediating efforts of the American government, which was trying to bring peace to both Namibia and Angola through the withdrawal of foreign troops from both countries.[189]

The Lusaka statement was adopted by a large majority of the annual general meeting of the SACC two months later, despite the fact that some of the delegates were unhappy about it. Two of them proposed a motion (which was heavily defeated) arguing that nobody could be 'compelled' to choose violence since it always involved choice. In abstaining, one of these delegates said, 'I could not vote for the implication that taking up arms is something in which one had no choice.' Another delegate was reported as saying he could not vote for the endorsement of the statement since it would mean the church endorsed violence, in which case, he said, 'I could never again preach about forgiveness and love.' Yet another priest said, 'Force should be permitted as a last resort. The odds must favour that the use of force will be successful. I don't think that every peaceful means has yet been used.'[190]

The Lusaka statement was the tip of an iceberg. The contribution by churches to violence goes back at least as far as the 'Kairos' document, which was signed by 150 clergy and theologians from 22 denominations in South Africa and published in 1985. The document said that a kairos – a moment of truth – had arrived for apartheid. 'Conflict and struggle' would have to intensify 'because there is no other way to remove the injustice and oppression.'

The document dismissed black moderates as 'collaborators' and argued that activities such as 'throwing stones, burning cars and buildings, and sometimes killing collaborators' ought not to be called 'violence' at all but rather self-defence since only oppressors might accurately be said to use violence. The document argued that it would be 'totally un-Christian to plead for reconciliation and peace before the present injustices have been removed'. Reconciliation was ruled out almost by definition: 'The conflict is between an oppressor and the oppressed...between two irreconcilable causes or interests in which the one is just and the other is unjust. The church must avoid becoming a "Third Force", a force between the oppressor and the oppressed.'

According to the second edition of the Kairos document, 35 000 copies of the first edition and tens of thousands of summaries in English, Zulu, Xhosa, Sotho, and Afrikaans were being distributed within a year, not to mention translations into foreign languages and worldwide distribution. An office was set up in 1986 to co-ordinate activities and initiatives arising from the document. In particular, efforts were made to 'empower Christian youth for more effective action within the church and society within the framework of the Kairos document'. In March 1986 a book of liturgies for Good Friday and Easter Sunday was published. The aim of one Easter sermon was 'to see the uprising of the people as the resurrection of Christ in South Africa today'. Revolutionary violence was thus not only endorsed but also equated with the resurrection, one of the central tenets of the Christian creed.

In July 1989, 539 South African theologians and other church people – some of them household names – issued a 28-page pamphlet called *The Road to Damascus: Kairos and Conversion*, which said that the only true Christians were those who adopted liberation theology. Again the document was translated into Afrikaans, Zulu, and Sotho, along with study guides, one aimed at a general audience, the other at students.

According to the Kairos line of thinking, 'There is a long and consistent Christian tradition about the use of physical force to defend oneself against aggressors and tyrants. In other words there are circumstances when physical force may be used. They are very restrictive circumstances, only as the very last resort and only as the lesser of two evils.'

These 'very restrictive circumstances' did not obtain in South Africa, however, for the society had already begun to change, most notably through the recognition of trade union rights for Africans on 1st October 1979 – as long ago as six years prior to the Kairos document. Six years before that, Africans had won the right to strike. Both of these important victories over the apartheid system were won by non-violent means. In June 1985 the Prohibition of Mixed Marriages Act and Section 16 of the Immorality Act were repealed. There were also strong indications in 1985 that the pass laws were on their way out. Job reservation was eroding, the Group Areas Act was crumbling, along with educational apartheid, home-ownership was being phased in, and Mr P W Botha had announced in early 1985 that independence would no longer be forced upon homelands. In short it was clear that the apartheid system was disintegrating.

In 1986 the pass laws were repealed. Leasehold was replaced by homeownership in the same year, and Mr Botha announced that the government accepted an undivided country and one citizenship and that Africans would be allowed to participate in government at executive level. The Restoration of South African Citizenship Act was passed. Yet a year later the Lusaka statement, in keeping with the Kairos document, implied that change could not come about except through violence.

The Kairos document, however, made it impossible for any of these reforms to be accepted as reforms. They were ruled out by definition on the grounds that 'reforms that come from the top are never satisfactory'. This is at best a half-truth. The legal rights to strike, to form trade unions, and to move from country to town were reluctantly conceded by the government because Africans created these rights for themselves by action on the ground. These reforms came from the 'bottom', not from the top.[191]

The government, however, was described as 'an enemy of all the people. A tyrant. A totalitarian regime. A reign of terror. The enemy of God.' Defined in these terms, 'the apartheid minority regime' was pronounced irreformable.

The churchmen thus did not merely issue one or two statements endorsing violence. They adopted a multi-pronged approach including:

- developing a theology to back their legitimation of violence;
- discrediting of reform;
- discrediting of non-liberation-theology minded Christians (who were branded as heretics and Satanists);
- spreading liberation theology through various languages into ordinary Christian worship; and

- targeting youth groups in particular to translate the Kairos document 'into action'.

Moreover, churches had the money to do this. Over the last ten or 12 years, tens of millions of rands have been given to the SACC and organisations linked to it by churches in other countries, mainly North American and European, and by the European Community. How much of this went to the promotion of liberation theology and how much into welfare or other projects is impossible to say, however.

How much influence did the churches have? The third impression of the Kairos document has the following to say in an appendix:

> 'The worldwide interest and excitement generated by this document has far exceeded anything the authors could have imagined even in their wildest dreams... The Kairos document has received extensive press coverage both in South Africa and overseas. Church magazines and newspapers have given it considerable attention and it has become a major topic of discussion in church conferences, synods, discussion groups and the like. Public meetings and seminars have been organised around it and committees are springing up here and there to plan action upon the reflections in this document.
>
> But most significant of all is the enthusiasm with which it has been received by very ordinary Christians in the black townships of South Africa. They are saying that the Kairos document gives articulate expression to what they believe as Christians about the present struggle for liberation in South Africa.'[192]

In a recent book entitled *Revolution or Reconciliation? The Struggle in the Church in South Africa*, Ms Rachel Tingle says that in countries like Britain, Christian allegiance is so low that the political pronouncements of church leaders would generally not have much practical effect. In South Africa, however, she argues, 77% of the population adheres to Christianity and church leaders command enormous respect. The book quotes one liberation theologian as saying that because of this, the theologies of liberation have been far more politically disturbing to South Africa than secular communism.

If the same ideas had been promoted in a form other than theology they would not have been taken seriously, but, presented in theological language, they were taken seriously.

An opponent of liberation theology, Bishop Bill Burnett, a former Archbishop of Cape Town, had the following to say in an open letter in December 1990:

> 'We have fiddled the scriptures for ideological ends, and it may be we must bear some responsibility for the awful breakdown of authority and random killings among young people, including policemen. We too need to repent. Bad government is better than no government and the terrible consequences of anarchy that must follow the breakdown of authority. This is a terrible thing to have done. In the light of this awful breakdown of authority in recent months, and the carnage that ensued, we may need to look into our own hearts, and to repent of our failure in leadership.'

'*The new Kairos*' was published by the Institute for Contextual Theology (ICT), a leading institution in the promotion of liberation theology, in September 1990. This document said that 'appeals for peace have more and more of a hollow ring about them because they do not put the blame where it really belongs – outside the townships'. It went on: 'The primary task at this moment, then, is not to call for peace but to call for justice.'

The statement that this was not the time to call for peace was made during a year of greatly intensified violence. It was made eight months after the release of political prisoners and the lifting of the bans on political organisations, four months after the signature of the Groote Schuur Minute (2nd May 1990) and the lifting of the state of emergency outside Natal, and a month after the signature of the Pretoria Minute, in which the ANC suspended the armed struggle.

In 1991, despite the political liberalisation set in motion the year before, the ICT said that it was developing a 'post-exilic theology' specifically to address 'the trends of "neutrality" and "reconciliation" creeping into the church'. In the same year, the ICT announced that a group of theological institutions around Pietermaritzburg in Natal were 'committed to providing a contextual theological education'. A publishing house was launched to provide the texts. Liberation theology was thus to be introduced into the curricula of seminars embracing the major Christian churches, both Roman Catholic and Protestant.[193]

Ironically, while the Kairos documents ignored all reforms, the South African Communist Party recognised them. It said in 1985:

> 'We may scorn the tricameral parliament as a farce, but we cannot dismiss as purely cosmetic, for example, the alterations in trade union law which have facilitated the development of the independent trade union movement and made it possible for African workers to organise legally, take part in collective bargaining and go on strike, albeit with many constraints. Nor can we oppose the scrapping of the Mixed Marriages and Immorality Acts, or the colour bar on the mines – the last refuge of job reservation, which Botha has promised to end by the beginning of 1986. And there are many other concessions of a similar kind which have been prised out of a reluctant regime by the mounting tide of internal and external pressure: freehold rights in the townships, freer movement of African labour in both urban areas and bantustans, the abolition of the Prohibition of Political Interference Act etc.
>
> It is true that all these "reforms"... affect only a tiny handful and leave the fundamental structure of apartheid intact – What then is their purpose? In our view they are clearly part of a strategy worked out by the Botha regime and its "constructive engagement" partners in the west to defuse the South African revolution.'

The SACP went on to quote Mr Tambo and the ANC as having 'alerted the people to the dangers of the enemy's strategy and called on them to intensify the fight'. In Mr Tambo's words:

> 'We charged them with the task to make the country ungovernable and to defeat the cunning enemy manoeuvre represented by the amended apartheid constitution. And to that call and that challenge our people have responded with unequalled enthusiasm, persistence and courage.'[194]

Liberation theology as expressed in the Kairos document necessitates portraying the state as an irreformable oppressor with whom there can be no reconciliation. If the state begins to reform and to seek reconciliation, the doctrine collapses. It is therefore necessary to find new ways of demonising the state. This is done by portraying it and its supposed allies as the sole causes of the violence in South Africa. Reports such as those of the Human Rights Commission (HRC), which seek to do that, describe the SACC as one of their 'subscribing organisations'. When liberation theology contends that violence against people alleged to be collaborators is not really violence, it is perhaps preparing the way for the HRC to be selective about the massacres on which it reports, ignoring those of people regarded as collaborators.

What some of the churches had to say about violence on the left was echoed on the right after the assassination of Mr Hani. Referring to one of the three people subsequently charged with the murder, the Boereweerstandsbeweging (BWB) said, 'The BWB does not accept that Mr [Janusz] Walus is a murderer or a terrorist, but a soldier and freedom fighter for the Boer people.' He had, said the BWB, emigrated from Poland to South Africa to 'rid himself of communism', against which he was a 'first-class fighter'. Echoing the attitude of people on the left with regard to revolutionary violence, friends of Mr Walus were quoted as saying his action was 'understandable'. The murder was an 'act of despair' by someone who had 'suffered under communism and fled his own fatherland and will find it hard to accept that the same fate may await him in his new country'.

Mr Piet Rudolph, who denied reports that he had supplied Mr Walus with the murder weapon, said, 'Like Mr Hani, I see myself as a freedom fighter.' The Afrikanerweerstandsbeweging said Mr Walus – who was one of its members – should be treated not as a criminal but as a political prisoner.[195]

Like the liberation theologians, the right defend their cause as the waging of a just war. Both argue in effect that the end justifies the means. Both forget the risks in such an approach, as spelt out, among others, by Professor Sir Karl Popper in his book *The Open Society and Its Enemies*:

> 'We must not think that the so-called "end", as a final result, is more important than the intermediate result, the "means". First, the so-called "end" is hardly ever the end of the matter. Secondly, the means are not, as it were, superseded once the end is achieved. For example, "bad" means, such as a new powerful weapon used in war for the sake of victory, may, after this "end" is achieved, create new trouble. In other words, even if something can be correctly described as a means to an end, it is, very often, much more than this. It produces other results apart from the end in question, and what we have to balance is not the past or present means against future ends, but the total results, as far as they can be foreseen, of one course of action against those of another.'[196]

Not all South African Christians, nor even all of those whose churches were affiliated to the SACC, agreed with the endorsement of 'force' as a means to end apartheid. It is possible that most rank-and-file Christians disagreed. A leading figure in one of the major denominations affiliated to the SACC has contended that the Lusaka statement was never endorsed by any of the churches affiliated to the council. The SACC, however, publishes a leaflet listing 21 member churches, a dozen associate organisations, three observer churches, and 24 regional and local councils of churches.[197] Whether intentionally or not, the list creates the impression that the SACC speaks for all the major Christian denominations and many minor ones other than three described as only 'observers' (among them the Southern African Catholic Bishops' conference). There is no indication in the leaflet as to whether the SACC always speaks for its member churches or not. Pronouncements by the SACC on violence and its determined – and continuing – campaign for economic sanctions against South Africa are undoubtedly two of the most important initiatives undertaken by Christian leaders in South Africa in the last decade. If, as has been suggested, the SACC did not speak for its member churches when it spoke on violence, the question arises, for whom did it speak? The same question arises with regard to the SACC's stand on sanctions. Even though most rank-

and-file Christians might have disagreed with the SACC on both violence and sanctions, it was not they, but the liberation theologians and the leadership of the SACC who made their views powerfully known and had the ear of the local and foreign press, the diplomatic circuit, and the international community. The African Independent Churches, which are said to enjoy the support of 35%–40% of South Africa's black population, are not even affiliated to the SACC.[198] Many ministers in various denominations that were affiliated no doubt disapproved of the endorsement of violence: some might have chosen not to contradict the SACC hierarchy, others might have been afraid to, for the 1980s were not an easy time for people to speak out against the left. The view, assiduously propagated by the left, that bannings, detentions, the state of emergency, and other measures had destroyed all opportunities for peaceful change in South Africa was powerfully held in press and diplomatic circles in the country, among many liberals and the intelligentsia, and was of course the prevailing wisdom abroad. Some liberals could – and did – muster cogent arguments against this viewpoint, but others did not want to hear them. On 9th May 1989, for example, the Institute issued a statement commemorating its 60th birthday which said, inter alia, 'The Institute continues to chronicle the horrors of apartheid, but it is careful not to perpetuate half-truths and myths about South Africa that erode both local and foreign belief in the possibility of peaceful transformation – *for example, the half-truth that all non-violent opposition to apartheid has been eliminated by the emergency regulations*.' The statement was reproduced in full in newspapers around the country, except for *The Star*, from whose version the italicised words were excised.

Stigmatisation

What some people regard as a just war against collaborators has its parallels in what others no doubt regarded as a just war against communists. Challenged in May 1992 on a television programme by a journalist, Mr Lester Venter, as to whether or not his government had ordered the killing of radicals, the then minister of defence, Mr Roelf Meyer, said 'No, a hundred times no.' The interviewer, having got Mr Meyer to admit that the ANC was considered the enemy, then wondered whether an 'enemy psychosis' was at work. Was it possible, he asked, that an instruction from the National Security Council to restrain certain political activists might – when it filtered down to the zealous men in uniform – be interpreted as an invitation to do their worst? Commented the *Sunday Times*: 'Meyer insisted no order could possibly be interpreted in that fashion. Maybe he is right. But Venter's proposition rings more depressingly true.'[199]

Indeed it does. To stigmatise people in this way risks being interpreted as issuing a licence to kill them. The object of all wars, just and unjust, is to kill the enemy. In fact, Radio Freedom explicitly called for the elimination of collaborators, puppets, sellouts, and the like. By hanging the deadliest of all political labels around its opponents' necks, Radio Freedom and others put them beyond the pale.

The process of stigmatisation has played a major role in the violence. It not only sets people up for attack but also scares off any would-be defenders. A stigma is a mark branded upon a criminal, a mark of infamy. The consequences of stigmatising people are strikingly shown in two studies of Nazi Germany which explain how it was that ordinary Germans kept quiet while the Nazis gassed the Jews. The books show that Hitler could not have got away with the gas chambers in, say, the mid 1930s, because public opinion would have been outraged. To get away with mass murder it was necessary first to stigmatise the intended victims. The start was a modest one, boycotting Jewish shops. Next, Jews were thrown out of social clubs. The process of social ostracism went hand-in-hand with anti-semitic propaganda. The two were mutually reinforcing. The severance of social ties meant that Gentiles no longer had any contact with Jews which might cause them to question the propaganda. Next, two or three synagogues were burnt down, so paving the way for Kristallnacht, when there was an orgy of arson against Jewish properties throughout the Third Reich. The arson was carried out by the Nazi activists. The rest of Germany kept quiet. The Nazis correctly interpreted this public acquiescence as a sign that they could get away with the next move... and so on. By the time the trains started moving to the death camps, Jews had been so demonised that when the rumours about the gas chambers started spreading, they did not cause any outrage, still less resistance, because public opinion no longer regarded Jews as human.[200]

The process of stigmatisation helps to explain why so many ordinary, decent white South Africans kept quiet for so long about bannings and house arrests and deaths in detention. When Miss Ruth Hayman, a Johannesburg attorney, was banned and house-arrested in 1966,[201] the organised legal profession refused to take up her case.[202] Mr Vorster had so stigmatised the liberals that most whites regarded them as communists and, when confronted with the injustice of banning without trial, retorted, 'Well she must have done something, otherwise Mr Vorster wouldn't have banned her.' This acquiescence paved the way for the next step – detention without trial, whose consequences have already been discussed.

As the Radio Freedom broadcasts made clear, stigmatisation of their opponents was a major strategy of South African revolutionaries in the 1980s.

The targets of stigmatisation included trade unionists. On 8th July 1984, *City Press* carried a headline 'I hate you, Lucy!' In letters more than an inch high, it quoted a president of the UDF, Mr Oscar Mpetha, as saying of Mrs Lucy Mvubelo, general secretary of the National Union of Clothing Workers, that she was 'one of the unionists who teaches workers that trade unionism does not involve politics but only bread and butter issues'. Speaking to 500 students at the fourth annual congress of the Azanian Students' Organisation, Mr Mpetha said that union leaders such as Mrs Mvubelo were telling workers they were not ready to revolt against apartheid, and so making them 'docile and subservient'.[203] On 17th July, the *Sowetan* reported under the headline 'Bombs hit Lucy's house' on the front page that two petrol bombs had been thrown through the window of her home in Orlando West (Soweto), completely destroying it (but causing no death or injury). The paper said that an anonymous 'South African Suicide Squad' had claimed responsibility for the bombing.

A few days later the *Sunday Times* reported:

> 'A new breed of terror is stalking the streets of Soweto – young thugs, armed with homemade petrol bombs, striking at the homes of the so-called "government

stooges" of black society. They call themselves the South African Suicide Squad, a sinister band which attacks carefully chosen targets in the middle of the night. At least three people, a woman and her two daughters, have burnt to death in a blaze. They have attacked 16 times, striking mainly at the homes of Soweto councillors. Each attack is always followed by a call to a local newspaper, claiming responsibility.'[204]

The South African Institute of Race Relations issued a press statement in which it said that remarks such as 'I hate you, Lucy!' fostered 'a climate in which attacks like that on Mrs Mvubelo are perpetrated'.[205] The spray of stigmatisation was spread very wide. The targets included long-standing opponents of the government who also opposed revolution, among them the South African Institute of Race Relations. As already noted, Ms Tingle's book shows also how liberation theologians stigmatised their more orthodox colleagues as apostates and heretics.

The process of stigmatisation may help to explain why the assassinations of IFP officials have received far less attention in the media than those of Dr David Webster and other anti-apartheid activists. Having been labelled as collaborators and therefore legitimate targets in a 'just war', IFP members could be murdered without prompting very much attention in the local and foreign media. While newspapers have printed vast numbers of articles about the 'third force' and assigned teams of reporters to expose criminal activity on the part of security forces or IFP members, the coverage of killings of IFP people has been minimal by comparison. The IFP claims to have lost 1 275 members and office-bearers since 1985, among them people killed in nine massacres in the last few months of 1992, 'mostly committed by trained hit squads in uniform'. So far as is known, no newspapers have mounted investigations into these killings, or into IFP claims that although Umkhonto we Sizwe might no longer be seen as a serious threat to white South Africa, it is 'a massive threat to that part of black South Africa which is not in the ANC camp'. IFP allegations that the government is turning a blind eye to members of Umkhonto being deployed from the Transkei in an 'unprecedented military offensive' to assassinate IFP leaders have also apparently not been investigated.[206]

After talks with the British prime minister, Mr John Major, in May 1993, Chief Buthelezi said Mr Major had been surprised when told of the scale of killings of IFP officials.[207] Three years previously, Chief Buthelezi had admitted that his reputation both at home and abroad had been tarnished by the IFP's involvement in violence: 'We have certainly paid a high price. The great superiority of the ANC has lain in its international diplomatic effort, and they have got the foreign press to swallow their version of events.'[208]

Liberal acquiescence

The growth of the culture in which some black people were mobilised to use violence against other black people occurred at a time when many liberals abandoned their traditional watchdog role and accepted the revolutionary agenda – that politics was of only two kinds, liberatory and collaborationist, and that those, like the Institute, advocating non-violent change, were naïve. Township residents have reaped the whirlwind sown by these simplistic notions. It is both tragic and ironic that black people, the victims of the apartheid system, should also be the main victims of the violence engendered by some of the liberatory strategies. Members of the liberal community who abandoned their old values – of non-violence and tolerance, of standing up for the underdog – may be said to have failed South Africa in her hour of need. In the 1960s they spoke up bravely for the rights of communists against the arbitrary powers of Mr Vorster. In the 1980s they failed to speak up for the rights of black policemen or councillors – even corrupt ones, who presumably have a right to a fair trial instead of being assassinated or summarily executed. Worst of all, they failed to speak up for ordinary people against the coercive strategies of revolutionaries.

The liberal intelligentsia failed even to speak up for freedom of speech on the once liberal English-speaking university campuses, which remain no-go areas for speakers to whom some white and black students object.[209] Coercion has indeed flourished in a climate where it has become acceptable in some intellectual circles. The then editor of *Business Day*, Mr Ken Owen, was widely condemned in liberal circles in Johannesburg when he wrote critical articles about the disappearance of free speech from the once liberal campuses.

While some liberals condoned the use of violence, others seemed reluctant to take the ANC's commitment to insurrection seriously. Mr Owen thus wrote in 1986 that ANC members in Lusaka had complained that liberal whites in South Africa constantly tried to soften their message. Referring to a press conference given by Mr Tambo, Mr Owen wrote:

> 'Tambo's comments were less widely threatening than government media pretended, but the commitment to "armed struggle" – to violence – is also more implacable than most liberals care to admit.'[210]

Despite the fact that the pattern of actual violence in the 1980s correlated closely with the type of violence called for by the ANC, some academic observers took the view that the 'people's war' amounted to little more than rhetoric.[211]

The slideaway of the 1980s has extended into the 1990s. Indeed, there remains at the time of writing a reluctance among liberals and in business, media, academic and political circles to even entertain the possibility that the continuing high levels of violence in South Africa may be attributable less to any 'third force' than to continued adherence to revolutionary strategies, if not always as official policies of organisations as a whole, then at least in the attitudes and behaviour of some of their component parts.

Summary: theories about violence

It may be appropriate to pause here to evaluate the two main theories put forward to explain political violence in South Africa. The 'third force' theory and its variants relies on considerable circumstantial evidence, apparently widespread belief, plausibility, and 40 years of National Party misrule. It sees a contradiction between Mr de Klerk's stated objective in constitutional negotiations and his actual behaviour and thus implies that he has a Machiavellian double agenda.

The theory put forward in this study relies on an agenda openly adopted by the ANC in the liberation struggle against apartheid. It does not see the march on Bisho as an aberration but as part of a plan to eliminate strategically placed rivals. Unlike the 'third force' theory, it does not put 30 years of black resistance strategies into George Orwell's 'memory hole'. It takes seriously the ANC's claim to be a revolutionary organisation, and it makes the point that revolutionary strategies provoke counter-revolutionary forces among both blacks and whites – a risk that appears to have been overlooked when these strategies were implemented.

To put the difference another way, the 'third force' theory looks at violence with one eye firmly closed. The theory put forward in this study tries to show, firstly, that violence emanates from both left and right, and, secondly, that a vicious circle of attack and counter-attack is part of the reason why violence continues.

Unlike the 'third force' theory, the theory in this study helps to explain violence against the ANC as well as violence against the IFP, along with violence emanating from and used against hostel residents, black councillors, the police, and the state itself.

Reports of agencies such as Amnesty, the International Commission of Jurists, the Human Rights Commission and the Community Agency for Social Enquiry are not helpful because, while they rightly castigate the IFP and the police for their involvement in violence, they turn a blind eye to the whole question of ungovernability and people's war. At best the recent reports of these agencies are one-sided and simplistic, at worst they amount to disinformation. Nor are these four the only agencies involved. There are others in South Africa, not to mention many abroad. Their efforts have been mutually reinforcing and magnified a thousandfold by the uncritical way in which many newspapers in South Africa and abroad have given splash coverage to their reports.

Whether intentionally or not, disinformation would serve a strategic objective of demoralising all security forces and disarming some of them. Such a strategy would involve, first, the unleashing of a people's war which plunges the country into violence and provokes a violent backlash; then the mounting of a propaganda war to blame all the violence on the state; thirdly, demands for the disarmament of all opposition forces. This objective has already been partly achieved.

The SADF's 31 battalion was thus formally disbanded on 7th March 1993, while members of 32 battalion were being placed elsewhere prior to the disbandment of that unit.[212] Both battalions had been the focus of criticism from a number of organisations, among them the ANC.[213] Two police units also criticised by the ANC, Koevoet and Askaris, were also disbanded.[214] Yet South African intelligence sources were reported in April 1993 as saying that more than 12 000 members of Umkhonto we Sizwe were undergoing training in various countries. The ANC refused to comment on the numbers, but confirmed that recruits were being trained in Uganda, Tanzania, and India. The intelligence sources were reported to have listed Cuba, Libya, Egypt, Ghana, Zimbabwe, and the Transkei as places where smaller numbers were also being trained. The ANC denied that training was taking place inside South Africa.[215]

Conclusion

Despite massacres in Natal earlier in the month, by the end of March 1993, the level of political violence in South Africa had dropped – from more than eight killings a day in 1992 to four a day in 1993. These lower levels had not been seen since the upsurge in December 1989. There was no more talk of Leipzig options. Although the Bisho shootings had provoked renewed calls for mass action, it did not materialise. The strategy appeared to have been shelved, which may be one of the reasons why the level of political violence had dropped. Whereas nearly 100 people died during the anti-VAT stayaway in November 1991, an increase in the VAT rate from 10% to 14% from 7th April 1993 provoked only token protest. There was no more talk of marches upon Ulundi – which had caused Chief Buthelezi to say, 'If the ANC [alliance] say they are coming to Ulundi to topple me and the government when there is already so much anger in the area because so many of our people have died at their hands, I say that will only make this low-intensity civil war escalate into a bigger civil war.'[216]

Most significantly, perhaps, the ANC had begun to accept at least part of the responsibility for violence instead of blaming only the government and its 'surrogates'. As recently as December 1992 Mr Mandela had said that 'the state security services, using certain black organisations, have been responsible for the death of no less than 15 000 people since 1984' (which means all of them). Where there were 'difficulties' with Umkhonto we Sizwe, it was the result of 'infiltration by government agents'.[217] Speaking in Mamelodi near Pretoria in April 1993, however, he said: 'I'm not going to blame the IFP and the government only. We must face the truth – our people are just as involved in violence.' Those involved in the senseless killing of innocent people, particularly the aged and children, were 'animals'. ANC supporters found guilty of participation in violence would face the 'strongest disciplinary action' or even dismissal from the organisation. Mr Mandela added there had to be political tolerance: violence could not be used against others except in self-defence. Organisations such as the IFP should be allowed to do their political work.[218]

The significance of this statement is that it was the first time Mr Mandela had publicly admitted the involvement of his own organisation (rather than simply a few 'misguided individuals') in violence. Mr Hani had similarly admitted only to 'tsotsi elements'.[219] Given his explicit references to children and the IFP, Mr Mandela's statement appears to have been prompted by the murder of six children – among them three sons of an IFP branch chairman – when the bakkie in which they were travelling to school was ambushed in the Table Mountain area near Pietermaritzburg on 2nd March 1993 by men wielding rifles and AK47s. Two men admitted by the ANC to be members of the organisation subsequently appeared in court in connection with these murders. Four other men suspected of involvement were thought to have gone to the Transkei.[220] A few days after the these killings ten people were shot dead when a minibus carrying commuters was ambushed about ten kilometres from the site of the massacre. A few days after that, four members of the ANC were killed when a bus carrying them to the hearing in connection with the massacre of the schoolchildren was itself ambushed at Wartburg.[221] Two men, evidently IFP supporters, were subsequently sentenced to death for the minibus massacre, the judge stating that neither of them had 'any reason to believe anyone in the bus had anything to do with the killing of the schoolchildren or, indeed, that they were supporters of the ANC rather than Inkatha'.[222]

Describing the killers as 'animals', Mr Mandela said at the time that the massacres were deliberate attempts to increase the supposed hostility between his organisation and the IFP. He blamed 'state security services' for fomenting violence.[223] A fortnight later, however, as we have seen, Mr Mandela accepted that the ANC was also responsible for violence. His admission that the ANC is just as much to blame for violence as the government and the IFP is of course a clear repudiation of the theories seeking to blame only the government and its 'surrogates'.

In an interview with the South African Institute of Race Relations about a fortnight later and about three weeks before he himself was murdered, Mr Chris Hani also commented on the Table Mountain killings:

'We were jolted by the massacre of the children, the ten people in the minibus, as well as the armed ambush of a bus of ANC supporters. The people of South Africa were shocked and horrified. The churches, the people, the ANC, and SACP, Inkatha, the international community. We said it was the work of animals. The same words were used by Mandela and Buthelezi. We visited the areas worst hit. It hit us in the face like a cold blizzard when we saw the destruction of villages, the stopping of ordinary life... We must move with speed. We are saying to ANC people that they must talk to Inkatha people on the ground. They must not wait until the big talks begin. We say to them that Inkatha is not your enemy, we are all victims of apartheid. Disagreements should not lead to physical fights... We must pursue the strategy relentlessly, even if we get another atrocity next week.'[224]

He also said:

'Because Inkatha has the KwaZulu police we can't defeat them militarily. Inkatha also cannot defeat us. We are in a no-win situation and so are they. That development has sobered people in both Inkatha and the ANC alliance.'

A few days before his assassination, Mr Hani criticised the Pan-Africanist Congress (PAC) for continuing armed struggle. Reacting to a statement by the Azanian People's Liberation Army (Apla) that 1993 would be the 'year of the great storm' in which Apla would step up the armed struggle,[225] Mr Hani said:

'I don't accept people calling for war and I don't accept the PAC's talks of the years of the great storms, because I feel we have achieved something in this country where those who oppressed us in the past are actually talking to us and showing readiness to negotiate for democratic elections.'[226]

Mr Hani referred in particular to 'the ambushing of ordinary white kids and women along some of the highways'. This was a reference to killings the previous month at Eikenhof, south of

Johannesburg, in which a mother and two children were killed by men with AK47s. The PAC was initially blamed for the killings, but two men subsequently charged with murder were admitted by the ANC to be members. They pleaded not guilty.[227]

Mr Hani's reference to the outrage over the Table Mountain killings is significant. This was the first time the media and influential religious organisations had paid much attention to killings when the IFP was the victim. As already noted, organisations like the Human Rights Commission had avoided even mentioning a previous massacre of about 30 IFP members in its study of massacres. Two journalists have pointed out that other massacres of IFP supporters have been virtually ignored by the local and foreign media.[228] The IFP had on several occasions criticised the South African Council of Churches (SACC) for one-sidedness in its attitude to killings. One IFP official said that the SACC never sent representatives to the funerals of IFP members, but always to funerals of ANC supporters.[229] After an attack on a hostel in which IFP members were killed, the official said, 'You won't see churchmen come to visit this hostel to offer comfort to the inmates there. These people are nothing to our church in South Africa.'[230] 'Our members have died in their hundreds. Not once did the SACC rebuke the actions of the killers. But...press statements by top SACC officials are issued to pay homage to the ANC dead.'[231] Another official attacked the Archbishop of Cape Town, the Most Rev. Desmond Tutu, and the general secretary of the SACC, Dr Frank Chikane, for their 'appalling display of selective empathy' by visiting some scenes of mass killings but not others.[232]

After the six children had been killed, however, Archbishop Tutu and Dr Chikane visited the site to offer their sympathy to the victims' families.[233]

If Messrs Mandela and Hani were speaking in more reconciliatory tones after the massacre than in the past, the same was true of Chief Buthelezi. In September 1992, following the massacre of 12 people en route to a conference of the Inkatha Youth Brigade in Ulundi, he told the youth that unless they 'bugger up the ANC, they are going to bugger up you and your future'. He was himself thus using against the ANC 'killing talk' of the kind he had previously accused the ANC of using against his own supporters. Some years before that he had said that if people wanted to fight 'dirty' the IFP would do so as well. On another occasion he had said that while Zulus asserted their right to pursue non-violent strategies, 'if some force an eye-for-an-eye and a tooth-for-a-tooth philosophy on us, then they will see that this philosophy settles easily on our shoulders when we are confronted with enemies who give us no choice'.[234]

In his address at the funeral of the six children, however, Chief Buthelezi urged his supporters not to avenge the deaths.[235]

Earlier Chief Buthelezi had also admitted the involvement of the IFP in violence. Speaking at a prayer breakfast in Durban on 7th March 1990, he said, 'Although I have not orchestrated one single act of violence... as the leader of the IFP, I know that the buck stops right in front of me.'[236]

The Bisho catastrophe and the Table Mountain killings may have been turning points – the former for the strategy of insurrection, which failed and was widely condemned, even by ANC sympathisers,[237] the latter for the unprecedentedly even-handed outrage at the murderous conflict in Natal. Perhaps too, as the ANC and the South African Communist Party (SACP) contemplated the approach of the day when they would be in government, they feared inheriting an ungovernable country, which realisation necessitated efforts to lead their supporters away from these strategies. The threat of violence from Apla and the white right helped to drive home the realisation that the country should be pulled back from the brink of a catastrophic slide into racial violence before the point of no return was reached.[238]

Perhaps Mr Hani's calls for peace shortly before his death were one of the reasons why there was not more loss of life in the wake of his assassination on 10th April. Many of the youths who went on the rampage regardless were probably acting under the influence of his earlier calls for a people's war. As Simon Schama wrote in his recent study of the French Revolution, 'The dilemma for successive generations of those politicians who graduated from oratory to administration was that they owed their own power to precisely the kind of rhetoric that made their subsequent governance impossible.'[239]

ANC officials were shocked by the violent behaviour of many

younger people when Mr Hani was assassinated. At least ten people were killed and more than 500 injured in what the *Sowetan* described as 'a day marked by chaos as thousands of people heeded a work stayaway call to honour Mr Hani'. Youths went on the rampage in several cities despite the efforts of ANC marshals to control them. In Cape Town, a senior ANC official was assaulted when he tried to control a rampaging mob. In America, television viewers were shocked at scenes of Mr Nelson Mandela being jeered at and booed at a memorial service for Mr Hani on 14th April in the Jabulani Stadium in Soweto, while the president of the PAC, Mr Clarence Makwetu, received a 'tumultuous welcome' and was 'cheered to the echo'. In the US, the UK, and Germany – and no doubt elsewhere – questions were asked as to whether the ANC could in fact control black youth.[240] A Natal Midlands ANC official said ANC leaders had tried to placate an angry crowd but 'one has to consider the anger of the people on the ground...we tried our best but we could not contain their anger'.[241]

Commenting on the Jabulani service, *The Weekly Mail* said: 'The biggest ovation' was reserved for the radical young lions of the ANC's youth league, who openly called for the townships to be made ungovernable, town councils to be forced out of their positions, and the 'boers to be made to pay for this atrocity.'[242]

The secretary general of the ANC, Mr Cyril Ramaphosa, said that given the grief and the large crowds 'the casualties have not been too numerous, and the chaos that broke out in one or two areas has not been so extensive that one can say the whole day was disastrous'.[243] During marches in various city centres a few days later, ANC marshals were more successful in keeping the peace. Granted extra powers of arrest, the marshals had done an excellent job, according to a Democratic Party MP, Mr Rupert Lorimer, who helped co-ordinate peace-keeping operations.[244]

Asked to comment on the booing of Mr Mandela, Mr Ramaphosa said the ANC had picked up signals that people ultimately held the National Party government responsible for Mr Hani's death.[245]

The youth had, however, picked up the signals from some of Mr Ramaphosa's own most senior colleagues. Mr Joe Slovo, national chairman of the SACP, said that the minister of law and order, Mr

Hernus Kriel, had refused requests from Mr Mandela for a police bodyguard for Mr Hani after attempts and threats to his life, an allegation denied by Mr Kriel, who said Mr Hani had been offered protection but had refused it.[246] In a leaflet – barely mentioned in the press – calling for a stayaway to mark Mr Hani's death, the ANC, its youth league, the SACP, and the Congress of South African Trade Unions (Cosatu) urged: 'Let us send a strong message to the racial minority that it will not kill our people and get away with it... Comrade Chris was killed by the system of apartheid... We put the blame for his death on De Klerk's shoulders. We believe that his murder is part of the plan to use violence to weaken the ANC–SACP–Cosatu alliance and defeat the struggle for freedom.'

The media focused much attention on the leader of the ANC youth league, Mr Peter Mokaba, when he led a rally with chants of 'Kill the boer, kill the farmer.' Mr Mokaba said that the youth should prepare for war and 'lay their hands' on those who had killed Mr Hani.[247] ANC officials repudiated these remarks and said that the organisation's songs about killing 'boers' would be reviewed.[248] However, at Mr Hani's funeral at the FNB Stadium in Soweto on 19th April, Mr Mandela made it clear that he held the government responsible for Mr Hani's death. Mr Hani's murder was no 'aberration', he said, but was consistent with past 'unsolved' assassinations, such as those of Dr Webster and Mr Goniwe. Mr Mandela went on:

> 'There has been a deliberate and massive propaganda offensive against Umkhonto we Sizwe, its cadres and leadership. No effort has been spared to criminalise both MK and Chris Hani. This has deliberately created a climate of acceptance when an MK cadre is assassinated, as dozens have been over the past months. To criminalise is to outlaw and the hunting down of an outlaw is regarded as legitimate. That is why, although millions of people have been outraged at the murder of Chris Hani, few were really surprised. Those who have deliberately created this climate that legitimates political assassinations are as much responsible for the death of Chris Hani as the man

who pulled the trigger, and the conspiracy that plotted his murder. In this regard, the minister of law and order and the chief of the army both have a great deal to answer for.'[249]

Thus, in the same speech in which he blamed criminalisation by the government for Mr Hani's death, Mr Mandela himself came close to criminalising the government. Mr Mandela was clearly riding a tiger because in the same speech he implicitly reaffirmed his own commitment to negotiations. But while he was doing so, youths outside the stadium were chanting 'Kill de Klerk,' and setting fire to nearby houses, killing two whites in the process.

None of this is in any way surprising. Mr Oliver Tambo, then president of the ANC, had been questioned about the youth by *Newsweek* in September 1985: 'Many of the present demonstrators are very young, even schoolchildren. Can you control what they do?' He answered: 'At this distance we cannot control events on an hour-to-hour or day-to-day basis. But we have called on the people in general to make the country ungovernable and apartheid unworkable, and what is happening is a response to that call... We can't tell our children that what they are doing is very dangerous. They are sustained by a hatred of the system.'[250]

The following year a black journalist in South Africa wrote that he had met members of the 'comrades', which his newspaper described as a faceless organisation sowing fear and terror in townships throughout South Africa.[251] At about the same time a white South African journalist, Mr Allister Sparks, wrote that

> 'A Khmer Rouge element is emerging in the black townships of South Africa that is beyond anyone's control, an element so brutalised that it now seeks only to kill and burn in blind revenge. This happens when situations of violence and repression become endemic with no prospect of a political solution in sight... Sixty percent of the black population of South Africa is under 16. That is the size of the Khmer Rouge we are creating... Now the ANC is losing control over them. Tomorrow they could be ruling over us.'[252]

Mr Sparks added that the authorities 'seemed blind' to what had caused the 'Khmer Rouge' problem:

> 'Stubbornly the government refuses to recognise that there is a pervasive sense of grievance and anger running right through the black population. It clings to the belief that the unrest of the past two years is all the work of Moscow-controlled agitators, who are infiltrating the country from outside and stirring up trouble by exploiting a few local grievances and intimidating the mass of the people.'[253]

A black journalist, Mr Jon Qwelane, saw things differently. Commenting on the murders of two black journalists and the attempted killing of a white journalist in the aftermath of the Hani assassination, he wrote:

> 'We bred the evil monsters who not only murdered Thusago and maimed Saunders, but also pumped five bullets into the body of another newsman, Sam Msibi. We bred and nurtured those monsters, because we chose to condemn violence only when it was convenient – expedient, perhaps? – to do so. We must stand condemned, every one of us. The so-called "children of the lost generation" have been allowed free rein to get away literally with murder because we made them something special – they were pathetic and hapless victims of a vicious apartheid system, soldiers in a moral war, brave young lions at the forefront of the struggle, children of broken families, and all that tommyrot. We are now reaping the whirlwind of the wind we sowed...'[254]

A second black journalist, Mr Phil Molefe, wrote:

> 'The black community is reaping the whirlwind of hailing ten-year-olds as "young lions"... Once regarded as the foot-soldiers of the liberation movement, the "young lions" have been allowed to claim too much power.'[255]

And another black writer, Ms Nomavenda Mathiane, said:

> 'Political organisations have created monsters they cannot control. In the interests of mobilisation, they gave the children the power to disrupt life – they used them to enforce boycotts, work stayaways, etc. etc. and having tasted that power, they are not about to give it up. These children are now a threat to democracy.'[256]

Many other black writers had written this some years before, as already noted. But far from the problem being confronted, the 'third force' theory was allowed to intervene. Just as Mr Sparks wrote that the authorities had 'hopelessly misread the situation in South Africa by blaming the unrest on Moscow-controlled agitators', so many journalists, politicians, and others misread the problem of the 1990s and sought to blame all the violence on a 'third force' conspiracy. Mr Sparks himself wrote in 1991 that he was 'concerned this violence is not driven from the grassroots level'. It was, he suggested, the work of professionals in the police and the 'informal military sector' on the right.[257]

The demonisation of the state and the romanticisation of the behaviour of its victims – two sides of the same coin – have helped to prolong the violence. By casting *all* the blame for violence on the state and throwing a smokescreen over the behaviour of the 'young lions' and other revolutionaries, demonisation and disinformation have done immeasurable harm to South Africa. Ecclesiastical and intellectual endorsement of violence helped to remove moral constraints from human behaviour and so may have contributed as much to the general escalation of crime and violence in the 1980s and 1990s as did economic stagnation and the brutalities of apartheid. At the time of writing both stereotypes were increasingly being seen for what they were. That in itself will enable the problem of violence to be dealt with more realistically, for the ANC had itself found in the wake of Mr Hani's murder that, far from being capable of manipulation like a switch or a tap, violence once turned on was very difficult to turn off.

References

1 For information on sabotage, 'armed struggle', and the measures taken to stop them, see Murriel Horrell, **Action, Reaction, and Counter Action – A Brief Review of Non-white Political Movements in South Africa,** South African Institute of Race Relations (SAIRR), Johannesburg, July 1971, passim; and **Surveys.**

2 John Kane-Berman, *Soweto – Black Revolt, White Reaction*, Ravan Press, Johannesburg, 1978, p219.

3 **Fast Facts** 1/93, 5/93, 7/93. The figures are based on a monitor of police, press, and other reports maintained by the Institute.

4 Calculations based on Institute research and the *Annual Report of the Commissioner of the South African Police*, RP 68/1992, pp99–101; *Hansard* 7 q cols 560–561, 16–19 March 1993; *The Citizen* 12 May 1993; 1983 **Survey,** p568, **Fast Facts** 1/93, 3/93, 5/93.

5 **Fast Facts** 4/92, 8/92.

6 Colleen McCaul, **No Easy Ride, The Rise and Future of the Black Taxi Industry,** SAIRR, Johannesburg, 1990, pp87–88; Commission of Inquiry Regarding the Prevention of Public Violence and Intimidation (the Goldstone Commission), *Second Interim Report on the Violence in the Taxi Industry*, Pretoria, 2 July 1992, p1.

7 1959–60 **Survey,** p58.

8 Shireen Motala (with contributions by Frances Potter), **Behind Closed Doors: A Study of Deaths in Detention in South Africa between August 1963 and 1984, and of Further Deaths between June 1984 and September 1985**, SAIRR, Johannesburg, 1987, table after p17.

9 Kane-Berman, **Soweto,** p9; 1977 **Survey,** p168.

10 Mona de Beer, *Who Did What in South Africa*, AD Donker, Johannesburg, 1988, pp74, 134.

11 In 1972, for example, the Institute was one of four organisations investigated by a parliamentary commission of inquiry set up after a debate on subversion (1972 **Survey,** pp52–53). Some Institute staff members refused to testify before the commission, in protest against the secrecy of its proceedings (1973 **Survey,** pp36–37). In the event, the Institute was

exonerated (although no charges were ever laid) (1974 **Survey**, pp38–39).

12 Many publications have gone out of print but at the time of writing the Institute had 135 in print.

13 For an analysis of the erosion of apartheid, see John Kane-Berman, **South Africa's Silent Revolution**, Second Edition, SAIRR, Johannesburg, 1991, passim.

14 The Goldstone Commission noted: 'The words "third force" have been used by many people in South Africa in many contexts and with no consistent meaning. The phrase has been used frequently with reference to a sinister and secret organisation or group that commits acts of violence in furtherance of some nefarious political aim' *Second Interim Report*, Cape Town, 29 April 1992). Some agencies that monitor violence do not actually use the term 'third force' but it is clear that they have a state-orchestrated plan in mind. A group called the Human Rights Commission (HRC) thus talks about a 'new total strategy' which is 'total because it incorporates the use of all the forces at the government's command, including the state security forces, vigilantes and hit squads...; total because it provides for simultaneous destabilising and undermining while engaging in negotiation' (*The New Total Strategy – Twelve Months of Community Repression, July 1990 – June 1991*, Human Rights Commission Special Report SR-11, Braamfontein, 1991, p19). The Community Agency for Social Enquiry (Case) and the HRC argue that there 'is clear evidence that the violence erupts at points when it most weakens the ANC and its allies, and dies down dramatically when it would most harm the government of F W de Klerk'. 'The violence appears to be switched on and off at strategic moments.' (Everatt D and Sadek S, *The Reef Violence: Tribal War or Total Strategy*?, Case/HRC material prepared for the International Commission of Jurists, Johannesburg, 28 March 1992.)

For the sake of convenience, this study uses the term 'third force theory' to embrace all theories that the state itself is orchestrating violence against its opponents as a matter of deliberate policy.

15 *Business Day* 8 October 1991; *The Guardian* 9 October 1991; *Sunday Times* 13 October 1991; Mr Mandela was speaking about the murder of Mr Sam Ntuli, general secretary of the Civic Association of the Southern Transvaal, on 29 September

1991 in Tokoza south east of Johannesburg. A committee of the Goldstone Commission subsequently reported that it could not come to any conclusion about Mr Ntuli's death. In July 1992 Mr Mandela was reported to have repeated his assertion that Mr de Klerk and his government were behind the violence in the country (*Sunday Tribune* 5 July 1992). On another occasion Mr Mandela said that he did not intend to suggest that Mr de Klerk was directly involved in the violence against black people (*The Star* 29 April 1992). Subsequently, Mr Mandela was reported to have said in Helsinki that 'it is a serious responsibility to accuse a head of state of himself fuelling the violence, the killing of innocent people, but facts indicate that De Klerk himself is involved in this'. An ANC official subsequently said Mr Mandela had been misinterpreted by a journalist who had difficulty with English, but the news agency which sent out the report was satisfied that this was not the case (*The Citizen* 23, 26 May 1992). Later Mr Mandela said his biggest criticism of Mr de Klerk was that he had failed to rein in the 'third force – elements in the security forces, military intelligence...a covert organisation working underground' and guilty of countless political killings, among them that of Mr Chris Hani (*Saturday Star* 1 May 1993).

16 Statement of the President of the ANC, Nelson R Mandela, at the United Nations Security Council, New York, 15 July 1992, pp5, 11; *Sowetan* 18 December 1992.

17 *Second interim report*, pp4–5; statement by Mr Justice R J Goldstone, Pretoria, 1 June 1992, p2; statement by Mr Justice Goldstone at the commission's preliminary hearing into the Boipatong massacre held at Pretoria on 6 July 1992, p4; see also **Fast Facts** 3/93.

18 *Finance Week* 17–23 September 1992.

19 Captain Mitchell and the four other policemen were found by Mr Justice Andrew Wilson to have attacked a house and to have killed six women, two children, and three men. Captain Mitchell was given 11 death sentences, while his co-accused were given terms of imprisonment (*The Citizen* 23 March 1991; *Cape Times* 17 October 1991, 24 April 1992; *The Star* 1 May, 7 May 1992).

20 *The Star* 26 June 1992.

21 *The Natal Witness* 6 May, 16 May 1992; *The Weekly Mail* 26 June–2 July 1992.

22 1991/92 **Survey**, ppxxxix, xl.

23 *Sowetan* 7 April 1993.

24 *New Nation* 8 May 1992; *Business Day* 2 March 1993.

25 Subsequent to the publication of the document, the minister of justice appointed the judge president of the Eastern Cape Division of the Supreme Court to reopen the inquest into the deaths of the four people in question, namely Messrs Matthew Goniwe, Fort Calata, Sparrow Mkhonto and Sicelo Mhlauli.

26 *The Citizen* 17 October 1992; *Sunday Tribune* 1 November 1992.

27 *The Star* 17 November 1992.

28 *The Star, The Citizen* 23 January 1993.

29 *Cape Times* 28 May 1990; *Sowetan, The Star* 2 August 1990; Mr Justice L T C Harms, *Report of the Commission of Inquiry into Certain Alleged Murders*, September 1990.

30 *Sowetan* 25 January 1993.

31 *Business Day* 17 November 1992; *Sunday Times* 20 December 1992; *Sunday Star* 20 December 1992, 16 May 1993; *The Citizen* 21 December 1992; *Beeld* 21 May 1993.

32 *Sunday Star* 24 January 1993.

33 *Beeld* 2 February 1993.

34 Republic of South Africa, *Report of the Commission of Inquiry into the Riots at Soweto and Elsewhere from 16 June 1976 to 28 February 1977* (the Cillie Commission), Volume 1, p522; Kane-Berman, **Soweto**, pp27–29; Anthea J Jeffery, **Focus on the Riot Police (Fast Facts** 7/91), SAIRR, Johannesburg, 1991. According to the Cillie Commission, 451 of the 575 people killed in the riots between 16 June 1976 and 28 February 1977 died as a result of police action. Kane-Berman gives a figure of 700 between June 1976 and October 1977. Assuming, in the absence of information to the contrary, that the same proportion of these were killed by the police as in the earlier period covered by Cillie (78%), then the number of people killed by the police in the Soweto upheavals was 546. If the 71 people killed at Sharpeville and Langa in 1960 are added to this total, along with 42 subsequent police killings listed by Jeffery, the total rises to 659.

35 Motala, table after p17.

36 1991/92 **Survey**, pxxix; *Hansard* 12 q col 1096, 19–23 April 1993.

37 **Fast Facts** 6/91; *Sowetan* 7 February 1991.

38 1992/92 **Survey**, ppliii, 294–295; Goldstone Commission, *second interim report*, p10; Goldstone *Boipatong statement*, p9.

39 *Switching off simplistic theories of violence – Paul Pereira puts the case against Case*, **Race Relations News**, February 1993, p9; *Business Day* 16 July 1992; *Finance Week* 17–23 September 1992.

40 *Sunday Times* 23 May 1993.

41 Human Rights Commission (HRC), *The New Total Strategy*, pp4, 19.

42 Anthea J Jeffery, **Spotlight on Disinformation about Violence in South Africa**, SAIRR, Johannesburg, 1992, pp43–44.

43 'Vigilante groups' were defined by the HRC as 'reactionary forces that arose out of the attempts of homeland administrations and black local authorities to defend their vested interests against their rejection by the communities in which they are located' (*Area Repression Report*, September 1992, HRC, p1).

44 *Institute queries human rights vigilante report*, **Race Relations News**, April 1991; HRC, *Human Rights Review* – South Africa 1992, Braamfontein, pp19–20; *Monthly Repression Report*, Braamfontein, February 1993, pp10–11.

45 *HRC Special Briefing on Massacres*, Braamfontein, July 1992.

46 Kim Hodgson: *A Synopsis of the Violence at Richmond*, 8 April 1991; *The Natal Mercury* 1 April 1991; *The Natal Witness* 1 April 1991; *Sowetan* 2 April 1991.

47 For more detail on the HRC report see Jeffery, **Spotlight on Disinformation**, passim.

48 *The Citizen* 15 October 1991.

49 Jacques Pauw, *In the Heart of the Whore: The Story of Apartheid's Death Squads*, Southern Book Publishers, Johannesburg, 1991, Annexure A, pp270–303.

50 *The Natal Witness* 27 April 1991; *The Natal Mercury* 12 June, 10 September, 23 September1991; *New Nation* 9 August 1991; *The Star, Business Day* 17 March 1992.

51 *Rand Daily Mail* 21 March, 22 March, 3 April, 31 May 1984.

52 *The Citizen* 27 August 1992; *Sowetan* 29 April 1993.

53 Jeffery, **Spotlight on Disinformation**, p12.

54 **Fast Facts** 9/92.

55 International Commission of Jurists, Geneva, press release embargoed for 29 March 1992; Jeffery, **Spotlight on Disinformation**, p13.

56 Inkatha Freedom Party, monthly report of known incidents of violence committed against IFP members and supporters since the signing of the peace accord on 14 September 1992, as of 30 June 1992, statistical data; *The Citizen* 3 June 1991; 1991/92 **Survey**, pxxxvi; statement by Chief Mangosuthu G Buthelezi at a conference on violence, Pretoria, 24 May 1991; address by Chief Buthelezi at Vosloorus Peace Rally, 21 March 1993; IFP, *Death List – Office-bearers and party leaders of the IFP assassinated in political violence*, undated but published in April 1993; opening statement by Dr F T Mdlalose, national chairperson of the IFP, to the negotiating council on Monday 26 April 1993.

57 **Fast Facts** 7/91; *The Citizen* 21 April, 15 September 1992; *Die Burger* 24 July 1992; *Business Day* 13 July, 14 July 1992, 5 January 1993; *Sowetan* 27 July 1992; and information supplied to the Institute by the South African Police.

58 *The Weekly Mail* 10–16 July 1992.

59 Address by Mr Anton Harber, co-editor of *The Weekly Mail*, to a meeting of the American Chamber of Commerce in Southern Africa, Johannesburg, 7 August 1992.

60 *The Star* 14 August 1992.

61 1967 **Survey**, p62. The laws in question included the Suppression of Communism Act of 1950 and the Terrorism Act of 1967 (Murriel Horrell, **Race Relations as Regulated by Law in South Africa 1948–1979**, SAIRR, Johannesburg, 1982, pp216, 227–228).

62 During the 1970s it was discovered that the government had secretly funded a newspaper, *The Citizen*, and other activities of the Department of Information (1978 **Survey**, pp3–5; 1979 **Survey**, pp7–10). In 1991 it was disclosed that secret payments to finance two Inkatha rallies had been made and that an Inkatha-related trade union had also received covert funding (1991/92 **Survey**, pliii). Earlier covert activities also involved an attempt by the Bureau for State Security (BOSS), using secret payments, to unseat Chief Buthelezi by setting up a rival party, Umkhonto Ka Shaka (Shaka's spear) (*The Star* 16 March 1993).

63 Cillie Commission: see also 34 above.

64 1985 **Survey**, p545, and subsequent **Surveys**, passim.

65 *Finance Week* 12–18 April 1990.

66 Kane-Berman, **Soweto**, pp11, 17, 31.

67 *Witness Echo* (supplement to *The Natal Witness*) 21 February 1991.

68 *Daily Telegraph* 2 December 1985.

69 **Fast Facts** 9/92; *The Citizen* 5 December 1992, 22 April 1993; *The Star* 17 May 1993; *Sunday Times* 23 May 1993; *Business Day* 27 May 1993.

70 Articles by Lawrence Schlemmer, Ernie Wentzel, and John Kane-Berman, **Race Relations News**, October 1983.

71 Address by John Kane-Berman to Business International Corporation, New York, December 1985, for example.

72 **Towards a Climate for Negotiation**, SAIRR, Johannesburg, November 1984.

73 Kane-Berman, **Soweto**, pp112–114, 120, 127, 130; Paul Pereira, **Coercion, Boycotts, and Stayaways**, SAIRR, Johannesburg, 1992, passim.

74 Jill Wentzel, **The Liberal Slideaway**, SAIRR, forthcoming.

75 1984 **Survey**, p77.

76 *Sowetan* 12 April 1985, 9 July 1985.

77 Wentzel, **Slideaway**.

78 This incident was reported by an office-bearer in the Democratic Party.

79 These are a selection of incidents reported in various newspapers.

80 **Fast Facts** 5/91.

81 *Sowetan* 1 November 1991; *Business Day* 4 November 1991; **Race Relations News**, December 1991.

82 See for example *Sowetan* 4 August 1992.

83 UN observers were sent to South Africa in August 1992 following a report by the organisation's secretary general and a visit to the country by his special representative, Mr Cyrus Vance.

84 Information supplied to the Institute by a building society; **Race Relations News**, December 1991.

85 *Southern Africa Report* 19 June 1992; *The Weekly Mail* 5–11 June 1992; information supplied to the Institute by the South African Police, June 1990.

86 Lawrence Schlemmer, *Dimensions of Turmoil: Position Paper on Current Violence in South Africa* (*Policy Issues and Actors*, Volume 4 No 2, 22 May 1991), Centre for Policy Studies,

Graduate School of Business Administration, University of the Witwatersrand, Johannesburg, 1991, p7.

87 Jill Wentzel, **History of Attacks on Black Local Authorities**, SAIRR, Johannesburg, August 1991, p4.

88 Wentzel, **History**, p18.

89 Kane-Berman, **Soweto**, pp204–216.

90 Wayne Safro, **Special Report on Violence Against Black Town Councillors and Policemen**, SAIRR, Johannesburg, December 1990; Wentzel, **History**, passim; see also **Surveys**, passim.

91 *State of the Nation* (published jointly by *Sowetan* and *Vrye Weekblad*), May 1985.

92 **Fast Facts** 7/91.

93 1985 **Survey**, p546.

94 *Sowetan Sunday Mirror* 24 March 1985; *The Star* 27 March 1985; *Sunday Times* 31 March 1985; *The Citizen* 2 September 1987.

95 *Saturday Star* 21 April 1990.

96 *Sunday Times* 31 May 1992.

97 1991/92 **Survey**, p34; *Sowetan* 25 February 1991; *The Citizen* 18 March, 31 May 1991; *Saturday Star* 23 March 1991; *City Press* 21 July 1991, 3 March 1992; interview with Anthea Jeffery, 18 March 1993 (an abridged version of which was published by the Institute on 16 April 1993).

98 Colin Legum's *Third World Reports*, No. FX.1., 16 October 1985.

99 Radio Freedom Addis Ababa, *ANC Denies it is Advocating Racial War in South Africa*, 6 September 1985; BBC Monitoring, *Summary of World Broadcasts* (SWB), ME/8051/B/4–5, 9 September 1985.

100 *Daily Telegraph* 30 October 1985.

101 Wentzel, **History**, p15; **Surveys**, passim.

102 Wentzel, **History**, passim; Motala; **Surveys**, passim. See also Anthea J Jeffery, **Riot Policing in Perspective**, SAIRR, Johannesburg 1991.

103 1985 **Survey**, p483; *The Citizen* 21 April, 15 September 1992, 25 March, 1 April, 6 May, 25 May, 28 May 1993; *Die Burger* 24 July 1992; *Business Day* 13 July, 14 July 1992, 5 January 1993; *Sowetan* 27 July 1992; **Fast Facts** 5/93, 6/93; *Hansard* 3 q col 188, 15–19 February 1993; and information supplied to the Institute by the South African Police; Jeffery, Hani interview, 18 March 1993; *Business Day* 22 March 1993;

Jeffery, **Spotlight on Disinformation**, p32; **Race Relations News**, February 1993.

104 Excerpts from statement on anniversary of banning of ANC, read by Mr Thabo Mbeki on Addis Ababa Radio Freedom in English, 7 May 1985, BBC SWB, ME/7947/B/6–8, 10 May 1985.

105 Radio Freedom 21 May 1985.

106 *Africa Confidential* 3 July 1985.

107 ANC, National Consultative Conference, June 1985, *Commission on Cadre Policy, Political and Ideological Work, Internal Commission Report, Commission on Strategy and Tactics*, p17.

108 *Africa Confidential* 3 July 1985.

109 *Daily Telegraph* 30 October 1985.

110 Radio Freedom, interview with senior commander of Umkhonto we Sizwe in English, 7 December 1986, SWB, ME/8438/B/1–4, 10 December 1985.

111 Tom Lodge, *Financial Mail* 28 June 1985.

112 *Daily Telegraph* 2 December 1985.

113 *The Star* 26 October, 17 December 1986.

114 *Guardian* 4 August 1986.

115 Howard Barrell, *New Statesman and Society* 16 February 1990.

116 *The Weekly Mail* 21–27 March 1986.

117 *The Citizen* 3 June 1986.

118 Radio Freedom, *Tambo Calls on All South Africans to Fight Apartheid*, 17 September 1985, SWB ME 8061/B/9–11, 20 September 1985.

119 See John Kane-Berman, "The Angry Youth", in Tony Manning (editor) *Trends Transforming South Africa – Insights, Information and Ideas*, Juta, Kenwyn, 1991.

120 Radio Freedom, ANC Military Official on Concept of 'People's War', excerpts from remarks by Chris Hani, Commissar of the People's Army, 12 September 1986, SWB ME/8365/B/6–8, 16 September 1986; Radio Freedom, ANC radio on Schools Closure: *State of Emergency Has Failed*, 11 September 1986.

121 *The Star* 13 November 1985.

122 *City Press* 15 April 1990.

123 *Sunday Times* (London) 14 September 1986.

124 *Saturday Star* 7 July 1990.

125 Joint report of the meeting in Lusaka of the ANC, the UDF, and Cosatu on 6 June 1989, published in *The Star* 20 July 1989.

126 *The Citizen* 11 December 1989; *The Indicator* 12–25 December 1989.

127 SAIRR press release 24 April 1990; *The Argus* 9 March 1990.

128 Anthea J Jeffery, **Conflict at the Crossroads in Bophuthatswana**, SAIRR, 1993; *The Weekly Mail* 11–17 September 1992.

129 *The Citizen* 28 March 1992.

130 Colin Legum, ibid; Tom Lodge, **The ANC After Nkomati**, second impression, SAIRR, 1988, p7.

131 *Business Day* 14 May 1993.

132 According to the minister of law and order, 85 people were killed by insurgents and 79 insurgents were killed in 398 insurgent attacks in the nine years up to 31 December 1985 (1985 **Survey**, p541); **Fast Facts** 1/93.

133 For example, five civilians were killed in what was said by some to be the first major insurgent attack on a 'soft target', a shopping centre in Amanzimtoti (Natal) in December 1985. This followed the Kabwe conference in June of the same year, which authorised members of Umkhonto we Sizwe to attack civilians, or 'soft targets' (1985 **Survey**, pp540–545). In May 1983, however, 19 people had been killed by a car bomb in a busy street in the centre of Pretoria outside South African Air Force headquarters. Eleven of the dead were whites and eight black. Of the 19, four were military personnel (1983 **Survey**, pp569–570).

134 Safro, ibid; Wentzel, **Attacks**.

135 Press release dated 24 April 1990. (The total of 3 699 fatalities that year was slightly lower than the 4 000 predicted in the press release.)

136 **South Africa in Travail: The Disturbances of 1976/77** (evidence presented by the Institute to the Cillie Commission of Inquiry into the riots at Soweto and other places during June 1976), SAIRR, Johannesburg, 1978, p20.

137 Notes by John Kane-Berman for addresses in Amsterdam on 18 June and London on 19 June 1990.

138 *Finance Week* 12–18 April 1990.

139 *The Star* 7 August, 8 August 1990.

140 *The Weekly Mail* 10–12 August 1990.

141 Anthea Jeffery (editor), **Forum on Mass Mobilisation**, SAIRR, Johannesburg, 1991, p7; **Spotlight on Disinformation**, p32; **The Criticism is Unfounded**, SAIRR, Johannesburg, February 1992, p17; **Race Relations News**, February 1993.

142 *The Citizen* 1 February, 28 May 1992.

143 *The Citizen* 29 July 1992.

144 *New Nation* 14–20 August 1992.

145 Document of the ANC national executive committee dated 3rd September 1992.

146 *Business Day* 8 September 1992.

147 Independent Board of Inquiry, *Fortresses of Fear*, Braamfontein, 1992, p4; SAIRR, **Travail**, p20.

148 The earlier stayaway was on 4th, 5th, and 6th August, organised by the Soweto students' representative council. Roadblocks prevented buses and taxis from taking people to town; drivers were threatened; city-bound workers were stoned and forced to turn back; many of the 13 railway stations in Soweto were blocked off, and trains were stoned; vehicles were stopped by pupils shouting, 'city-bound cars belonging to betrayers who want to take a back seat during the struggle' (Kane-Berman, *Soweto*, pp3, 112–114).

149 Cillie, p135.

150 *City Press* 13 July 1986; *Business Day*, *Sowetan* 14 July 1986; and a record of incidents compiled by Judith Hudson of the research staff of the Institute.

151 Kane-Berman, **Soweto**, pp130–132.

152 *Sowetan* 15 March 1985.

153 *Sowetan Sunday Mirror* 19 May 1985.

154 Wentzel, **Slideaway**.

155 *The Weekly Mail* 9–15 January 1987.

156 Address by John Kane-Berman to a Conference on Crisis Intervention, Tara Hospital, July 1986.

157 Report of the second committee appointed to inquire into the violence at the President Steyn Gold Mine in Welkom, November 1991, passim.

158 *City Press* 3 June 1984; *Sowetan* 8 July 1985; *Sunday Star* 21 April 1991.

159 *Sowetan* 24 April 1991; *The Citizen* 23 April 1991, 29 April, 3 May 1992; *The Star* 29 April 1991; *Business Day* 29 April 1991; *Sunday Star* 21 April 1991; *Beeld* 1 May 1991; other press reports; and a memorandum from Mr Musa Myeni dated 30 April 1991.

160 *Sowetan* 25 June 1992.

161 *Sunday Times* 20 September 1992.

162 *The Citizen* 22 April 1993.

163 *The Weekly Mail* 30 August–5 September 1991.

164 *The Citizen* 3 August 1992.

165 *The Weekly Mail* 17–23 May 1991.

166 Press statement by Ms Suzanne Vos, Inkatha Freedom Party, 14 May 1991.

167 *The Citizen* 13 May 1991; *Business Day, The Citizen* 17 February 1993.

168 *Sowetan* 30 September 1991; *Saturday Star* 5 October 1991.

169 Report of the committee of inquiry into the phenomenon and causes of violence in the Tokoza area, under the chairmanship of Mr M N S Sithole, 17 November 1992, pp7, 9, 13.

170 *The Citizen* 15 May 1993.

171 **Fast Facts** 5/93; *The Citizen* 18 May 1993.

172 See a forthcoming study by the Institute.

173 *The Star* 24 January 1979; *The Star* 30 June, 1 July 1986; *Business Day* 1 July 1986. From 1977 onwards there were a number of insurgency attacks in KwaZulu, including attacks on police stations which some observers believed were designed to undermine support for Chief Buthelezi; in 1986 three people were killed and 48 injured when youths petrol-bombed busses carrying Inkatha supporters from a rally in Soweto.

174 See the Radio Freedom broadcasts referred to above.

175 PANA interview with Alfred Nzo, Lusaka, 4 July 1986; PANA dispatch from Dakar quoting Mr Oliver Tambo, 2 July 1986; 1986 **Survey**, p542.

176 Jeffery, Hani interview.

177 Anthea J Jeffery, interview with Mr Kim Hodgson of the Inkatha Institute violence monitoring unit, 5 March 1993.

178 *Sunday Times* 7 July 1985.

179 *Saturday Star* 5 October 1991.

180 Thami Mazwai et al, **Mau-Mauing the Media: New Censorship for the New South Africa**, SAIRR, Johannesburg, 1991, p14; and information subsequently supplied to the Institute, 1991.

181 *New Statesman and Society* 16 February 1990.

182 Safro; Wentzel, **Attacks**.

183 *The Star* 6 November 1991.

184 The number of necklace killings is as follows: 406 between September 1984 and December 1989 (information supplied by the South African Police in a letter to the Institute, June 1990); 1990, 48; 1991, 24; first six months of 1992, 23 – a total of 501.

185 *The Star* 29 May 1992; *The Weekly Mail* 29 May–4 June 1992.

186 *The Weekly Mail* 8–15 April 1993.

187 See, for example, the *Sunday Times* of 2 August 1992, in which the dean of St Alban's Cathedral in Pretoria says, 'The South African church has never, through the lips of any responsible or representative South African church leader, supported or aided in promoting this cause violently.'

188 *The Citizen* 6 February 1991.

189 1987/88 **Survey**, ppxxxiii, 526.

190 1987/88 **Survey**, p234; *The Star* 3 July 1987; *Ecunews*, August 1987, p3.

191 See Kane-Berman, **Silent Revolution**, passim.

192 *The Kairos Document – Challenge to the Church, A Theological Comment on the Political Crisis in South Africa*, various editions, 1985, 1987, passim.

193 Rachel Tingle, *Revolution or Reconciliation? The Struggle in the Church in South Africa*, Christian Studies Centre, London, 1992, pp83, 84, 94, 102–104, 111, 112, 114, 121, 122, 126, 127, 155–157, 160, 171, 196, 249–250.

194 Editorial notes, *The African Communist*, No 103, fourth quarter 1985.

195 *The Citizen* 12, 13, 14 April 1993; *Beeld* 13 April 1993.

196 K R Popper, *The Open Society and its Enemies*, 4th edition (revised), Routledge and Kegan Paul, London, 1962, volume 1, p287.

197 Statement made and leaflet handed out at a meeting at the Institute's offices on 29 March 1993.

198 **Race Relations News** February 1993.

199 *Sunday Times* 31 May 1992.

200 Milton Meyer, *They Thought They Were Free: The Germans 1933–45*, Chicago Press, Chicago and London, 1955, passim, especially pp55–56, 117–123, 166–173; William Sheridan Allen, *The Nazi Seizure of Power – The Experience of a Single German Town 1922–1945*, revised edition, Penguin Books, 1989, especially pp218–232.

201 1966 **Survey**, p67.

202 Information supplied to the writer by an attorney, Mr Louis Kane-Berman, who tried to persuade the profession to protest publicly on her behalf.

203 *City Press* 8 July 1984.

204 *Sunday Times* 22 July 1984.

205 Press release 24 July 1984.

206 Mdlalose op cit; *Ilanga* 26–28 March 1992; *Business Day* 9 September 1992; *Sunday Tribune* 6 December 1992; *The Citizen* 27 April 1993.

207 *The Citizen* 4 May 1993.

208 *The Times* 8 February 1990.

209 See for example, **Race Relations News**, October 1992; 1986 **Survey**, pp470–472, 477–478.

210 *Business Day* 16 January 1986.

211 See, for example, *Sunday Star* 20 September 1992.

212 *The Citizen* 10 February, 8 March 1993.

213 See, for example, *The Question of South Africa*, Report of the Secretary General of the United Nations, New York, August 1992, pp7–8.

214 *Business Day* 17 July, 4 August 1992; *The Star* 6 August 1992, 3 May 1993.

215 *Sunday Times* 11 April 1993.

216 *The Citizen* 21 September 1992.

217 *Sowetan* 18 December 1992.

218 *Business Day, The Citizen, Sowetan, Beeld, The Star* 7 April 1993.

219 *The Citizen* 1 December 1990; *Beeld* 7 July, 12 September 1992.

220 *Sowetan* 4 March 1993; *Business Day* 9 March 1993; *The Natal Witness* 16 April 1993; *The Citizen* 6 March 1993.

221 *Business Day*, *The Star* 9 March 1993.

222 *Business Day* 30 April 1993; *Sowetan* 3 May 1993.

223 *The Citizen* 13 March 1993; *Sunday Times* 14 March 1993.

224 Jeffery, Hani interview.

225 *The Citizen* 6 April 1993.

226 *The Citizen* 7 April 1993.

227 *Beeld* 4 April 1993; *The Citizen* 8 April 1993; *The Star* 14 April 1993.

228 Patrick Laurence, *The Star* 24 June 1992; David Beresford, *The Guardian Weekly* 11 September 1992.

229 *The Citizen* 25 November 1991.

230 *The Citizen* 22 June 1992.

231 *Sowetan* 4 October 1992.

232 *The Weekly Mail* 18–24 September 1992; *The Citizen* 19 September 1992.

233 *The Citizen* 5 March 1993.

234 *Sunday Tribune* 6 September 1992; 1983 **Survey**, p53; *International Herald Tribune* 30 September 1986; policy speech, March 1990, pp63, 74, 84–87.

235 *Sunday Star* 14 March 1993.

236 Mangosuthu G Buthelezi, address at the 18th KwaZulu Legislative Assembly prayer breakfast, Royal Hotel, Durban, 7 March 1990, p3.

237 Jeffery, **Criticism**, p17, gives examples.

238 Between the beginning of 1992 and the end of April 1993 there had been 434 attacks on people on white-owned farms and small holdings; in the first four months of 1993, 29 people had been murdered in these attacks (as against 16 in the comparative period the previous year). Some of these attacks were blamed on Apla. The PAC said attacks on white farmers by Apla – 'a disciplined organ of the PAC' – were legitimate because of the 'political crimes' they had committed, such as forcing people off their land. The increase in killings of white farmers and their families led to renewed attempts by white groups to mobilise opposition to what they saw as National Party capitulation to the ANC (*Beeld* 13 May 1993; *The Citizen* 20 May 1993; *Business Day* 25 May 1993).

239 Simon Schama, *Citizens – A Chronicle of the French Revolution*, Viking, London, 1989, p532.

240 *Business Day*, *The Citizen*, *Sowetan* 15 April 1993; *Beeld* 16 April, 17 May 1993; *Sowetan* 16 April 1993.

241 *Business Day* 15 April 1993.

242 *The Weekly Mail* 16–22 April 1993.

243 In 1976, when police shot dead marching schoolchildren in Soweto, the township erupted and within 24 hours a journalist wrote that 'he felt like a war correspondent flying over a city after a bomb attack'. In a little more than a week, at least 176 people had been killed. In striking contrast, reaction to the Hani assassination (on a Saturday) did not occur until the following Wednesday and was then in the form of calls for a stayaway and organised memorial services and calls for renewed mass action. The violence was on a lower scale than in 1976 (*The Citizen* 15 April 1993).

244 *The Star* 19 April 1993.

245 *The Citizen* 15 April 1993.

246 *Sunday Times* 11 April 1993; *Business Day* 19 April 1993.

247 *The Star* 22 April 1993.

248 *Sunday Times* 2 May 1993.

249 *Sowetan* 20 April 1993.

250 *Newsweek* 16 September 1985.

251 *Business Day* 30 October 1986.

252 *The Star* 17 September 1986.

253 *The Star* 17 September 1986.

254 *Sunday Star* 2 May 1993.

255 *Sowetan* 17 May 1993.

256 Speech in Italy, April/May 1993.

257 **Race Relations News**, December 1991.

South African Institute of Race Relations
Current Publications

Justice Richard Goldstone, *Do Judges Speak Out?* (1993)
Anthea Jeffery, *Conflict at the Crossroads in Bophuthatswana* (1993)
Anthea Jeffery, *Spotlight on Disinformation about Violence in South Africa* (1992)
Helen Suzman, DBE (Hon), *No Going Back* (1992)
Anthea Jeffery, *Riot Policing in Perspective* (1991)
Anthea Jeffery, *Forum on Mass Mobilisation* (1991)
Helen Suzman, DBE (Hon), *Holding the High Ground* (1991)
Ahmed Jooma, *Migrancy after Influx Control* (1991)
Thami Mazwai et al, *Mau-Mauing the Media: New Censorship for the New South Africa* (1991)
John Kane-Berman, *South Africa's Silent Revolution* (2nd edition, 1991)
Monica Bot, *The Blackboard Debate: Hurdles, Options and Opportunities in School Integration* (1991)
Anatoly Gromyko and John Kane-Berman (eds), *The Moscow Papers The USSR and South Africa: Similarities, Problems and Opportunities* (1991)
W J P Carr, *Soweto: Its Creation, Life and Decline* (1990)
Stanley Mogoba, *Harmony: Key to National Reconstruction* (1990)
Justice M M Corbett, *Guaranteeing Fundamental Freedoms in a new South Africa* (1990)
John Kane-Berman et al, *Beating Apartheid and Building the Future* (1990)
Harry Mashabela, *Mekhukhu: Urban African Cities of the Future (1990)*
Colleen McCaul, *No Easy Ride: The Rise and Future of the Black Taxi Industry* (1990)

continued

Mauritz Moolman, *From Town to Township: Regional Services Councils Assessed* (1990)

Steven Friedman, *Options for the Future: Government Reform Strategy and Prospects for Structural Change* (1990)

Stanley Mogoba, John Kane-Berman and Ronnie Bethlehem, *Sanctions and the Alternatives* (2nd edition, 1989)

These are available from:

The Bookshop
South African Institute of Race Relations
P O Box 31044
Braamfontein
2017 South Africa